TRUST FALL

TRUST
FALL

How the Fall of Man reveals
a God worth trusting.

BRENT FAULKNER

I pray that from his glorious, unlimited resources he will empower you with inner strength through his Spirit. Then Christ will make his home in your hearts as you trust in him. Your roots will grow down into God's love and keep you strong. And may you have the power to understand, as all God's people should, how wide, how long, how high, and how deep his love is. May you experience the love of Christ, though it is too great to understand fully. Then you will be made complete with all the fullness of life and power that comes from God. (EPHESIANS 3:16-19 NLT)

CONTENTS

Acknowledgements ix
Introduction xi

Part One – The Fall of Trust
1. In the Beginning 1
2. A Word About Trees 15
3. Deception 21
4. Distrust...31
5. Desire 41
6. Disobedience 55
7. Division 65
8. Death 73

Part Two - The Trust in the Fall
9. That, and More 83
10. Hide and Seek 87
11. God Doesn't Throw Away What's Broken 97
12. You Are What You Wear 109
13. Head Crushers 121
14. The Good News of Being Banned 131
15. Trust Foundation...143

Appendix..147
Notes...151

ACKNOWLEDGEMENTS

No book is written in isolation. This book was formed through the thoughts and contributions of others. Many of the ideas in this book have emerged through learnings from The Bible Project and The Bema Discipleship Podcast. These two tremendous resources have helped me discover the beauty of scripture and understand it in deeper ways. I'm indebted to my Tuesday night discussion group where many of these thoughts were wrestled through and lived out. I am thankful for Crossroads Community Church allowing me space to teach some of these early thoughts in studies and sermons. Thank you to Maggie, Jason, and Erin for insightful and helpful feedback during the writing process. I am thankful for Ethan and Eli, who as experienced readers, provided valuable feedback on the cover design and interior layout. And a big thank you to my wife, Addy, who has been my biggest cheerleader, sounding board, and crucial contributor through the whole process.

INTRODUCTION

Did Adam and Eve have belly buttons?
Where was the Garden of Eden?
Did snakes walk on legs before God cursed them?
Do men have one less rib than women?
Was creation literal 24-hour days or time periods?
What kind of fruit was the forbidden fruit?

As a pastor, I get asked all kinds of questions about the Bible, especially questions about the first few chapters of Genesis, the first book of the Bible. There's something about that ancient story that captures our imagination and piques our curiosity. I believe there are no bad questions about the Bible, but that doesn't mean every question we ask is created equal. Some questions are more helpful than others. Marty Solomon, author of *"Asking Better Questions of the Bible,"* says, "When we ask questions the Bible isn't trying to ask, we always get the wrong answers."[1] While "Did Adam and Eve have a belly button?" may be a valid question, it isn't a question the Bible asks or attempts to answer. So, any conclusion we draw just won't be helpful in getting us where scripture is trying to take us. The Bible is more concerned with helping us understand who God is and who we are in relation to him. Questions that help us discover those truths have a greater impact than other questions the Bible may not be trying to answer.

This book is my attempt to help us discover what the Biblical writers were trying to reveal about God and about humanity in the first few chapters of Genesis. We will pay close attention to Genesis chapter 3, the story of the Garden of Eden, and to what is commonly referred to as "The Fall of Man" in Western Christianity. The Christian circles I find myself in place a lot of emphasis on the Fall. It's referenced often in sermons and evangelism strategies, yet for all the times it is referenced, very few times are the events of Genesis 3 studied in an in-depth manner.

If the good news of the gospel is in response to this event described in the opening pages of Genesis, it might do us good to understand what the Bible is trying to say.

To do that, we have to overcome another challenge. Even though Genesis 3 isn't often studied in depth, the frequency with which we reference it creates a false familiarity. We think we know it. This is what Jewish Rabbi David Forman calls the "lullaby effect."[2] You know the classic lullaby, "Rock-a-bye baby in the treetop…" We sing it to babies as a soothing and loving song, but the lyrics are quite unsettling. "…when the bough breaks, the cradle will fall, and down will come baby cradle and all." We've sung those words so many times we fail to realize what they are really saying. In the same way, we can hear a scripture referenced so often that we fall asleep to its intended meaning. This is especially true for people who grew up in the church. We just assume we know all about a story in the Bible and don't study it further.

For all those reasons, I think we miss some fundamental truths the Scripture is trying to teach us about God's character in its opening pages. Not only do we miss those truths, but we also misinterpret and mischaracterize the heart of God. That can cause real damage. I've taught this content in several settings, and nearly every time, someone approaches me on the verge of tears and shares how they realized they had the wrong view of God because of how they've experienced these stories in their past. These mischaracterizations of God can cause us to question God and lose trust in him, which is the very thing I believe Genesis 3 is warning against.

I invite you to join me on this journey to take another look at the garden story in Genesis 3. We will look at the questions the text is trying to answer. We'll see how the Fall not only sets up the good news of the gospel but has good news in itself. We'll learn that the story of the Fall reveals a God worthy of our trust. We'll discover ourselves in the story. And hopefully, we will awaken from the lullaby effect and see this ancient story in new ways that speak to our lives today.

PART ONE

THE FALL OF TRUST

CHAPTER 1

IN THE BEGINNING

I enjoy the Star Wars saga. (I'll save you from debating which trilogy is better and in what order they should be viewed.) I think Star Wars movies have the best opening sequences of any movie franchise. I love the anticipation that builds the moment the text appears, "a long time ago in a galaxy far, far away." There's a moment of silence, then the theme song bursts into your eardrums. The opening crawl glides up the screen, giving you just enough information to set the context for what will unfold in the next couple of hours.

That's how the first half of Genesis functions in the Biblical narrative. But it's much richer and more informative than a few throw-away sentences on a movie screen. We learn so much about God's intention, his character, and his creation from the opening pages of the Bible. If we miss some of these key truths, we can miss the context of the story and the important character development of the main character.

As a pastor, I'm in a lot of settings where "gospel presentations" are given. In these presentations, communicators do their best to briefly but compellingly explain the good news of Jesus and its impact on the life of every human being. I have often noticed these explanations of the gospel begin by referring to the sinful state of humanity resulting from Adam and Eve's disobedience, which is often referred to as "the Fall." The beginning point for most of these gospel presentations is to start with the problem of sin.

I think beginning with the problem of sin is itself a problem. It can cause the gospel to come across like a sales pitch. Any good infomercial starts by emphasizing the problem and then offering its product as the solution. Many evangelism strategies focus on convincing someone they're a sinner and then presenting Jesus as the solution. That can unintentionally set up the gospel as a simple transaction instead of the beautifully good news it truly is. However, the most compelling reason for the gospel not to start with sin is because the biblical story doesn't start this way. Instead of starting with the problem of sin, the Bible starts by highlighting God's creative intent of blessing and goodness.

We'll talk about the problem of sin soon enough, but before we take an in-depth look at Genesis three, it will be beneficial to remind ourselves of how it all began. The Fall of

Man isn't the beginning of the story. Let's start by looking at the truth found in the creation stories of Genesis 1 and 2. Keeping these truths in the back of our minds will be crucial to helping us understand what is being communicated when we do encounter the Fall in chapter three.

I need to acknowledge there are entire books devoted to understanding these creation accounts in the opening paragraphs of Genesis. This story is rich in wonder and meaning. Perhaps foolishly, I'm only dedicating a chapter: the Star Wars opening crawl, if you will. I want to focus on a few key aspects that will help us set the stage for what we'll encounter in Genesis chapter three. Just know that we'll be barely scratching the surface.

GOOD

The biblical narrative opens with the account of how God created the heavens and the earth. What follows is a beautiful, complex, and highly structured poem describing how God brings order to the chaos of nothingness. God's creative actions are divided into days. In the first three days, God speaks and separates spaces. In the next three days, God speaks and fills those spaces with life. As you read through the creation poem, you begin to see repeated words and phrases. Pay attention to those. Ancient Hebrew writers used repetition to emphasize key points. These repeated words are important in understanding what is being communicated.

One of the words that appears over and over again — seven times actually — is the word "good."

What is described as good? Is God described as good? That would make sense.

Interestingly, God isn't described much at all in this account. We're told what God does, and we're told what God thinks about the things he has just created. God thinks they are good. He creates something, and when he looks at what was created, he sees it as "good."

Light?...Good.
Sky, land, and sea?...Good.
Plants?...Good.
Solar system?...Good.
Birds and Fish?...Good.
Land animals?...Good.
Humans?...

Now, this is where things get interesting. When God created humans in his image, he blessed them and then looked over all that he had made and saw it was not just "good," but *very* good." It's particularly interesting that this last statement is the seventh mention of the word. In Hebrew, the number 7 conveys the idea of completion or perfection. It's as if the author doesn't want us to miss this vital truth — all of God's creation is completely, fully, very...good. Before loss, before fear and hiding, before sin, there is an underlying intrinsic goodness in all things. Humanity is good. That's the start of the story. Let's not forget.

PARTNERS

We have a giant tub of Legos in my house. Years of kits given as birthday and Christmas gifts have been piled together in a beautiful mass of unlimited creative potential. One of my favorite things to do is sit down with my kids and just free-build together. The collaborative act of building with them brings me joy. Even though some of their builds early on weren't that great, technically speaking, I still treasured their participation. Today, I'm impressed by their creativity and what they dream up. I think we see a similar desire for collaboration from God in the creation accounts.

As you read through Genesis 1, the flow of the text seems to slow down on day six. It starts out like the previous days of creation as it describes the creation of animals, then the pace changes and describes the creation of humanity with more detail. The text uses phrases that aren't used to describe anything else in the creation story. It's as if the author is saying, "Hey! Don't miss this!"

Read through these verses and pay attention to what is repeated.

> Then God said, "Let us make mankind in our image, in our likeness, so that they may rule over the fish in the sea and the birds in the sky, over the livestock and all the wild animals, and over all the creatures that move along the ground."

So God created mankind in his own image,
in the image of God, he created them;
male and female, he created them.
God blessed them and said to them, "Be fruitful
and increase in number; fill the earth and subdue
it. Rule over the fish in the sea and the birds in the
sky and over every living creature that moves on the
ground." (GENESIS 1:26-28)

What did you notice?

A couple repetitive words and phrases I noticed…
Image: Humanity is created in the image of God.
Rule: Humanity is called to rule over the other living
creatures.
While much could be said about each of these ideas. I want
to focus on how these two ideas are connected. Notice what
verse 26 says, "Let us make mankind in our image, in our
likeness, *SO THAT* they may rule over…" Mankind's ruling over creation is connected to and dependent upon the
image of God.

Why does that matter?

The Hebrew word used for image is almost exclusively used
in the Old Testament to describe idols. When Genesis says
we are created in the image of God, it implies that we are
God's idols. What does an idol do? An idol functions as a
representation of a god and its character. It's a way for people

to connect with that god. And it represents the authority of that god. That's why idol worship was such a big deal in the Old Testament. People were submitting to the authority of false gods instead of the true God.

By creating humanity in his image and placing humans over creation, God was establishing human beings as his representatives. Humanity's intended role was to represent God to all of creation and to extend God's authority and goodness as they ruled and stewarded the rest of creation. God even invites humanity to participate in the creative act. The first two commandments to humanity are:

> Be fruitful and increase in number and;
> Rule over the other living creatures.

This is partnership language. God's creative intent was for humanity to function as his partners, continuing the creative process and stewarding the good creation around them.

This is emphasized again in Genesis chapter two, which is another telling of the creation account. God forms man from the dust of the ground, breathes life into him, and places man in the garden to *work it and take care of it*. We miss it in our English translations, but the Hebrew words translated as "work" and "take care of" are the same words that would later be used to describe the priest's role in the Tabernacle and temples.[1] It's as if the writer is describing Eden as a temple and humanity is intended to be God's partner, playing the priestly role of caring for creation and representing the creator to the creation. God even gave authority to man to name all the animals — an act of ordering creation. Again, partnership language.

These creation stories paint a picture of partnership, co-creation, and relational joy between God and the humans created in his image. It's as if God invites humanity to the pile of Legos and says, "Let's build something together."

NAKED

When you imagine the Garden of Eden in your mind, what do you see? Odds are you see a scene with a tree and a man and woman standing naked with leaves strategically placed so certain body parts aren't visible. It's an iconic scene that's been recreated in children's Bibles and stained-glass windows. What's interesting is the fig leaves don't appear until late in the story and then only for a short time. For most of their time in the garden, Adam and Eve were naked. Genesis chapter 2 ends with this statement, "Adam and his wife were both naked, and they felt no shame."

That's kind of an odd detail to include in the story, don't you think?
Were the Biblical writers anti-clothing?
What's going on?

This isn't about clothing or the lack of it. The Biblical writer is, in a poetic way, talking about the type of relationship between Adam, Eve, and God. When someone is naked, there is nothing to hide. Every part is fully visible. Most people will only choose to be naked in front of someone they deeply trust and have an intimate connection with. This phrase points to an intimate, trust-filled relationship. This is a community where there is nothing to hide. This isn't about physical nakedness. This is an emotional and relational nakedness. Everyone can fully be themselves, all while feeling no shame! Trust, vulnerability, and intimacy define their interactions.

As scary as it would be to stand naked in a room full of people, it is perhaps scarier to have all our secret thoughts, hidden motivations, and true opinions on display for all to see. Think about how much of ourselves remains hidden. We conceal certain aspects of our personality depending on who is around. We feel like we're not enough or like we're too much. We tell ourselves, "If they knew the real me, they wouldn't like me." So, we hide, pretend, overcompensate, and shut off parts of us — all at the expense of true relational connection. How many of our relationships are built on a façade? But not in the garden. Adam and his wife were naked, and they felt no shame. The start of the Biblical story reveals God's original intent for humanity is for everyone to be fully themselves, have nothing to hide, and be fully accepted. What a wonderful community that would be! To be fully known and fully accepted.

ABUNDANCE

Pop quiz: How many trees are in the Garden of Eden? Do you know? Let's read Genesis 2 and find out.

> Now the Lord God had planted a garden in the east, in Eden, and there he put the man he had formed. The Lord God made all kinds of trees grow out of the ground — trees that were pleasing to the eye and good for food. In the middle of the garden was the Tree of Life and the Tree of the knowledge of good and evil... (GENESIS 2:8-9)

> And the Lord God commanded the man, "You are free to eat from any tree in the garden; but you must not eat from the tree of the knowledge of good and evil, for when you eat from it you will certainly die." (GENESIS 2:16-17)

How many trees are in the garden?

Most people, when I ask that question, answer "one" or "two." Two trees are specifically identified. One of which is off-limits. But did you notice all the others? "God made *all kinds* of trees grow." These trees were "pleasing to the eye and good for food." This isn't some backyard garden. It sounds more like an orchard! What does God invite the humans to do in this orchard? "You are *free* to eat from *any* tree in the garden." God also gave free reign to all these trees. One boundary, though. For their own safety, they weren't to eat from one specific tree because it would kill them. Everything else was able to be enjoyed!

We tend to place a lot of our focus on the single off-limits tree. (Rightly so, as we'll discover in the chapters ahead.) But sometimes, we miss an important detail in the story. Every other tree was a free game — including the tree of life! They could eat from them, look at them, climb them, and enjoy their shade.

Genesis 2 paints a picture of abundance. There is more than enough. These trees were providing food and so many other good things. Adam and his wife were invited to enjoy them! God's creation provides more than enough. There isn't scarcity in the garden. There is abundance. Don't miss this. The original intent of God is to surround his image-bearing partners with blessing and abundance. God doesn't cut corners. He doesn't give second-rate things. He provides abundantly.

ORIGINAL INTENT

With our quick overview of Genesis 1 and 2, we discover that the story of the Bible doesn't start with sin and brokenness as many of us might think. The story is better than that. God's original intent is goodness, blessing, abundance, and intimacy with humanity. These truths reflect the beautiful character of God.

As we journey further into Genesis, don't forget these foundational truths laid out in the beginning of the story.

Good
God saw what he created as intrinsically good — you and I included. That means any sin or failure we experience isn't who we truly are but a deviation from God's intent. The foundation of our identity is that of God's beloved image-bearing partners.

Partner
God set humanity apart from the rest of creation to be his image-bearing partners to care for and continue his creation project. Our personalities, abilities, and passions aren't accidental. They're part of how God has shaped each one of us to reflect his goodness. Each of us is invited to partner with his will for the world.

Naked
God desires a trust-filled intimate relationship with every human being. There's nothing to hide. We are invited to be fully ourselves and experience full acceptance in God's presence.

Abundance
God has abundantly blessed humanity with more than enough. We are invited to enjoy his creation and live with open hands.

Don't underestimate what the creation story reveals about God's character. This isn't a fluke. This is the foundation that Biblical writers intentionally lay. God's character, as it's described in Genesis 1 and 2, ripples into the entire Biblical narrative. Let these truths be the start of your story as well. These things are true even when we fail to trust that they are.

CHAPTER 2

A WORD ABOUT TREES

When I was a kid, I entered my dog in the 4-H dog training program. His name was Domino, and he was a hyperactive Border Collie. He was one of those dogs that would chase his own tail in circles. During the training, we spent weeks practicing sitting, staying, laying down, and other such commands. Domino had mild success but never really stopped his tail chasing. One of the higher-level obedience tests was to command your dog to sit and stay, take a few steps in front, and place a treat on the ground. The goal was for the dog to remain sitting until the owner gave the command to eat. What a temptation for those dogs. You'd see every dog's eyes fixed on the treat. Only the best-trained dogs could pass that test. Eventually, the owner would give the command, and the dog would race to the treat for their prize. Domino failed that test every time.

When you read Genesis 2, it may seem odd that God would place a tree in the garden and then say, "Don't eat it."

Why would God do that? Was this some sort of obedience test for Adam and Eve? Was it a way to prove their worth and devotion?

At first glance, it may seem that God was trying to do the same thing with Adam and Eve that I was trying to accomplish with Domino. It may seem like God was just setting humanity up for failure. There has to be more to this tree.

First, let's remind ourselves what this tree was named. It is called "the tree of the knowledge of good and evil."

Well, that brings up another question. Why is the knowledge of good and evil off-limits? Wouldn't God want Adam and Eve to have knowledge of good and evil? If they were called to be God's partners ruling over creation, wouldn't it benefit them to know the difference?

All excellent questions. Pay attention to those seemingly odd things in the Bible. They're usually invitations to dig deeper. Understanding the meaning behind the tree of the knowledge of good and evil will help unlock the message this story is trying to communicate. It's more than just a simple obedience test. Let's look at this tree in light of what we already know from the story.

Remember that talk about partnership and nakedness? God desires a relationship with his image-bearing partners that is grounded in a trust-filled intimate community. One function of the tree of the knowledge of good and evil is to allow this trusting, intimate relationship to exist. True relationships are mutual. It takes two parties choosing to trust each other. If Adam and Eve had no choice in the matter, would it be a real relationship? God wants real relationships, not robotic obedience. That requires the ability to not reciprocate the love and trust that God extends. The tree of the knowledge of good and evil represents that choice. By allowing the possibility for Adam and Eve to not choose trust, God was allowing trust to truly exist in their relationship. Placing the tree in the garden wasn't simply an obedience test. It allowed for free will, and it was an invitation into a partnership of love and trust.

Another aspect of the tree's name sheds light on what this story is trying to communicate. It is the tree of the *knowledge* of good and evil. That seems to imply Adam and Eve didn't have knowledge of such things. However, in the story, they do have knowledge of good and evil. God has already communicated what was good and what was not good. In Genesis 1, God spoke over and over about what is good. In Genesis 2, God spoke about what wasn't good; "It's not good for man to be alone." The knowledge of good and evil has already been provided by God. So, the prohibition against the tree isn't God's attempt to keep Adam and Eve ignorant. Instead, it shows God's desire that *he* be the only source defining what is good and what is evil. The tree of the knowledge of good and evil represents a choice that each one of us has to make. Will we trust God's definition of good and evil, or will we eat from the tree and choose to define good and evil in our own eyes or from some other perspective? Again, we see God's heart for a trust-filled intimate relationship with humanity. We are invited to trust that God sees reality as the clearest. We're invited to trust in the Lord with all our hearts and not lean on our own understanding. (Proverbs 3:5)

Let's talk for a moment about knowledge. There are two different types of knowledge. There is *intellectual* knowledge, and there is *experiential* knowledge. They are not always the same thing. For example, when I was in middle school, I got a three-wheeler (an ATV with three wheels). My mother pleaded with me to be careful because three-wheelers can be dangerous. My angsty response was always, "I know, mom." I intellectually understood. But that didn't necessarily lead to wise decisions when operating the three-wheeler. One day, I was racing my friends (who had four wheels on their ATVs). I hit a big rut, the three-wheeler flipped, and I went flying through the air Superman-style, resulting in a broken ankle and some good road rash. I now had *experiential* knowledge.

When Genesis talks about knowing good and evil, it is referring to experiential knowledge. God never intended humanity to *know* evil, that is, to know it experientially. God knew if humanity failed to trust his wisdom about what is good and what is evil, they might define it by another standard. Since God is the creator of the universe, any other understanding of good and evil would go against the grain of reality, and when you go against the grain, you get splinters. Much of the pain we've experienced in our lives can probably be traced back to our own or someone else's choice not to live in line with God's definitions of good and evil. God desires to see humanity flourish as we choose to trust him, not just intellectually but experientially as well.

When intellectual knowledge and experiential knowledge meet, it's called wisdom. God wants humanity to have *his* wisdom. Wisdom is the right application of knowledge. For example, it would have been wise for me to trust my mom's knowledge and apply it to my actions. I foolishly did not. Wisdom is a big deal in the Bible. God intended mankind to have wisdom. And wisdom comes from God. Interestingly, Proverbs 3 connects wisdom to the other tree in the garden — the tree of life. That tree wasn't off-limits. Adam and Eve were free to eat from it.

> "Blessed are those who find wisdom,
>   those who gain understanding...
> She is a tree of life to those who take hold of her;
>   those who hold her fast will be blessed."
> (PROVERBS 3:13, 18)

God wants his image-bearing partners to have wisdom — to know how to rightly apply the knowledge he provides.

This proverb reminds us that God's wisdom brings life and flourishing. It is the life-giving tree that is freely available for Adam and Eve to eat from.

God desires his wisdom — his definition of good and evil — to be the guide for you and me. And when it comes to that kind of tree, there is abundance. There is more than enough if we choose to trust it.

So, the tree of the knowledge of good and evil is not some sort of obedience test where God is trying to train us like I tried to train my dog. It's far more. The tree of the knowledge of good and evil is an invitation into a trust-filled intimate relationship with God. It represents every person's choice to trust God's wisdom and live to our full potential. What will you choose?

In the first two chapters, we journeyed through Genesis 1 and 2. We've seen glimpses of God's character and his intent for humanity. The world God created is marked by abundance, intimacy between creator and created, and God's wisdom as the guiding path. What could go wrong?

On to an in-depth look at Genesis 3.

CHAPTER 3

DECEPTION

Now, the serpent was more crafty than any of the wild animals the Lord God had made. He said to the woman, "Did God really say, 'You must not eat from any tree in the garden'?" (GENESIS 3:1)

When my boys were young, I'd let them have soda as a treat. They were always excited to drink the carbonated, caffeinated, high fructose corn syrup-infused beverage. At their age, a full can was too much, so I'd divide it up between the two of them. It became a bit of a ritual. I would set two glasses on the table. They'd get their faces close to the glasses. I'd crack open the can and start pouring it into one glass, then the next. With each pour, the soda would bubble and fizz. The anticipation on my boys' faces would grow. With utmost care, I would evenly divide the beverage, ensuring each boy got an even amount. Once the last drop came out of the can, the boys were free to enjoy their treat. Now, you might think this scenario would end with two happy boys enjoying their sodas. You'd be wrong.

More often than not, as they'd reach for the glasses ready to drink, one of them would say, "He got more." With those three little words, the mood would instantly change. All enjoyment would cease as they examined the two glasses for any imperceptible difference. All the most sensitive scientific equipment cannot compare to the accuracy of a child's eye! Somehow, he noticed a difference. He concluded one glass had more. The kitchen table would then turn into a courtroom interrogation.

"Why did you give him more?"
"He has more, it's not fair."
"I need more."

I'll spare you the details of how the conversation typically devolved. It often ended in some of my less-than-stellar parenting moments.

Something caused a perspective change for my son. Something got into his head and changed the way he interpreted the situation. Something caused him to focus on what he didn't have instead of what he did have. I call that something "perception deception."

Perception deception is a perspective shift that causes you to see abundance as scarcity and blessing as affliction. There are two parts to perception deception. First, there is something that shifts the focus from abundance to scarcity. My son had six ounces of delicious beverage in front of him. But instead of seeing a treat to enjoy, all he could focus on was the tiniest bit he had less. Secondly, what is intended as a blessing is seen as an affliction. This drink was supposed to be a treat. A loving gift from his generous father. Instead, this became a perceived injustice, causing him to question the intent of his father — "Why did you give him more?" It was as if there was premeditated ill-intent behind the half-a-drop less received. (I still maintain they were exactly the same!)

Perception deception is not just something little boys with soda experience. It's something we all experience. In fact, it's as old as the Garden of Eden.

As the Genesis story continues into chapter 3, a strange, unexpected character is introduced. We're told about a crafty serpent that talks to Eve. If you're reading the story with fresh eyes, you should be asking, where did this serpent come from, and why is it talking? Pretty strange, huh? Unfortunately, the serpent is another casualty of the lullaby effect.[1] Those who have grown up with this story referenced over and over don't think about how random and strange the introduction of a talking serpent is in the flow of this story. But it is strange. It should catch our attention. An animal that is crafty and that talks? This clearly isn't an ordinary snake. But let's not dig into what or who the serpent is just yet.

Right now, let's focus on what the serpent said…

> "Did God really say, 'You must not eat from any tree in the garden'?"

Is that what God said?

Nope.

Here's what God said…

> "You are *FREE* to eat from *ANY* tree in the garden; but you must not eat from the tree of the knowledge of good and evil, for when you eat from it you will certainly die."

We learned in Genesis 1 and 2 the garden was a place of abundance. Many trees were freely available. Adam and Eve were invited to enjoy them all. Only one was off-limits. A forest of trees to use. Just one that is unavailable.

But then a serpent appears. We're told this serpent is crafty. Its question is not innocent. The serpent has an agenda. What is it trying to do with the question?

I think this is an act of perception deception. The serpent is trying to shift Eve's focus. Instead of seeing the abundance of God's provision, the serpent wants to deceive Eve into seeing scarcity. "Did God really say you can't have any of these trees?" The serpent doesn't flat-out contradict God. It just asks a question. But it's not a neutral question. It's the kind of question that gets in a person's head and changes how they see reality. Scarcity instead of abundance. Affliction instead of blessing. It's a subtle shift that can have major implications.

FROM ABUNDANCE TO SCARCITY

If you're like me, "not enough" is a constant thought sitting in the back of your mind.
Not enough time.
Not enough money.
Not enough sleep.
Not enough space.
Not enough talent.
I'm not enough.

Perception deception produces a "not enough" mindset. Even more challenging, the world we live in reinforces this message. Our entire economic system is built on the "not enough" mindset. Perception deception is at the core of any good marketing campaign. Advertisers work hard to convince you that what you have is not enough and they have the product that can give you what you need. A scarcity mindset sells more products. Technology companies operate on "planned obsolescence." Companies specifically plan and design products with a limited life or frail design, so they will become obsolete. They ensure there won't be enough storage, memory, or updates forcing you to upgrade to the newest model. Politicians get elected because of scarcity mindsets. They spin any data point possible to show that our current situation is bad, but a vote for them will make it all better. We live in a world that constantly tries to convince us there is not enough.

As a scarcity mindset takes hold, it has negative effects not just spiritually but mentally and physically as well. Researchers at Harvard and Princeton teamed up for a study and discovered that a scarcity mindset makes your brain operate less efficiently. Active concern about perceived scarcity consumes "mental bandwidth" and keeps your brain from devoting brain power to things like planning ahead and problem-solving. This keeps a person stuck and can reinforce self-defeating actions.[2]

KJ Ramsey, a licensed professional counselor and author, talks about how scarcity impacts us emotionally and physically.

> "Scarcity sinks us into physiological states of stress that can keep us stuck living out stories of self-protection and striving instead of kindness and joy.
>> Maybe if we had more possessions, we'd feel like we belong.
>> Maybe if we had more power, we'd feel safe.
>> Maybe if we could prove our worth, we'd finally be loved.

You can't will your way out of the wounds of scarcity that speak into your story every day. You can't preach your way to the peace you need. Scarcity will keep being a scary, self-fulfilling prophecy that can never be satisfied by reaching for possessions, power, and perfect faith — until we acknowledge its presence in our physiology, reach for its roots, and tend to its shoots. The truth is that scarcity is a story that lives in your body. And if you don't reckon with scarcity, it will rule you."[3]

The land of scarcity has such a negative impact on us because we were never created to live there. Instead, God invites us to live in the land of enough. This invitation is expressed in Jesus' model of the Lord's prayer — "Give us today our daily bread." It's an invitation to trust that God will give us what we need for this day. Today, there is enough.

FROM BLESSING TO AFFLICTION

My very first car was given to me by my grandparents — I didn't have to pay anything for it. It was a 1987 Buick Skylark station wagon. My grandparents drove it, my uncle drove it in college, and it was passed on to me. Let's just say the car was well-loved by the time I got the keys. It was speckled with rust. The radio antenna was broken and held together with a pencil and duct tape. The back taillight was busted and taped over. The fabric on the ceiling was falling and held up with thumbtacks. Yet, with all the imperfections, it was my own car and a generous gift from my grandparents. I was proud to have that car. Well, that was until my friend's parents bought him a brand new shiny red Chevrolet Camaro with T-tops for his 16th birthday. Suddenly, my grandparent's gift didn't seem so generous. What once seemed like a blessing now appeared like a burden when it was parked next to that red Camaro.

That's the danger of perception deception. It can cause us to misinterpret blessings as affliction. Perception deception becomes a distorted lens that twists everything good into a negative. This has real damage to relationships. It kills gratitude and joy.

If perception deception were like a fire, then comparison is gasoline. When we constantly compare ourselves to others, we rarely become joyful, generous, or pleasant to be around. Comparison results in a scarcity mindset when we perceive we are less than, or it results in pride if we perceive we are more than. Either result takes us away from who God created us to be.

Perception deception is particularly damaging to our view of God. We can lose sight of God's abundant love and turn to false beliefs about God's character. "God must not care. God must not be present. God must be angry with me and is waiting to punish me." These false beliefs ultimately erode the relationship that God desires to have with us.

So, what about you?

Where is perception deception at work in you?

Perhaps you have a fear there won't be enough, so you hold on to what you have a little tighter and view everyone else as competition. Maybe you have a sense of injustice that someone got something you deserve. Why did they get promoted over you? You work harder than anyone else. Maybe there's an underlying worry that God is holding out on you. Why did that person's prayers seem to get answered when it seems your prayers are falling on deaf ears?

The serpent's deception begins a turn in the Genesis narrative. Perception deception is the first step in a path that leads to the breakdown of trust between humanity and God. It's also at work turning our hearts and minds today. We're presented with two views of God: that of Genesis chapters 1 and 2 and that of the serpent. Which will you believe? Is God trustworthy in his promises of abundance and blessing, or is there not enough?

We must cling to the truth of the garden. There is enough. You are enough. God created you for partnership. There's nothing to prove. No amount of clawing your way to the top will change how God feels about you. Your possessions, performance, and power don't define your worth. You can release your grip. God is in control. He is good. You can trust him.

Of course, as we will see with Eve, this is much easier said than done.

CHAPTER 4

DISTRUST

The woman said to the serpent, "We may eat fruit from the trees in the garden, but God did say, 'You must not eat fruit from the tree that is in the middle of the garden, and you must not touch it, or you will die.'" "You will not certainly die," the serpent said to the woman. "For God knows that when you eat from it your eyes will be opened, and you will be like God, knowing good and evil." (GENESIS 3:2-5)

The Muppet Show introduced the world to iconic characters like Kermit the Frog, Miss Piggy, and Gonzo. I watched reruns as a kid. A couple of my favorite characters were Statler and Waldorf, the cantankerous old men who sit up in the theater balcony giving their opinions. In one episode, I remember they started to heckle the performers...

STATLER: Boo!

WALDORF: Boooo!

STATLER: That was the worst thing I've ever heard!

WALDORF: It was terrible!

STATLER: Horrendous!

WALDORF: Well, it wasn't that bad.

STATLER: Oh, yeah?

WALDORF: Well, there were parts of it I liked!

STATLER: Well, I liked a lot of it.

WALDORF: Yeah, it was GOOD, actually.

STATLER: It was great!

WALDORF: It was wonderful!

STATLER: Yeah, bravo!

WALDORF: More!

STATLER: More![1]

It's comical how, comment after comment, they talk themselves into a different opinion. This makes for good comedy, but it's also a reflection of the serpent's question at work. Perception deception has a way of changing our focus in small, subtle steps. But it's not just losing sight of abundance and blessing that hurts us. The biggest casualty of perception deception is trust.

Let's take a look at Eve's response to the serpent. At first glance, she seems to hold her ground. She corrects the serpent's misleading question. But look a little closer. There are a few subtle differences.

This is what God originally commanded.

> "You are free to eat from any tree in the garden, but you must not eat from the tree of the knowledge of good and evil, for when you eat from it, you will certainly die."

Now read Eve's statement to the serpent.

> "We may eat fruit from the trees in the garden, but God did say, 'You must not eat fruit from the tree that is in the middle of the garden, and you must not touch it, or you will die.'"

Notice any differences?
The differences are subtle, but they matter.

1. God said, "you are *FREE* to eat from *ANY* tree in the garden…" Eve leaves out "free" and "any." It seems Eve deemphasized God's abundance by just saying, "we may eat fruit from the trees in the garden."
2. God stated the consequence of eating the fruit strongly, "you will *CERTAINLY* die." Eve leaves out "certainly" and simply states, "you will die." It seems Eve is deemphasizing God's warning.
3. The biggest difference is Eve's addition of a prohibition. She adds, "And you must not touch it." God never said they couldn't touch it, only that they couldn't eat it.[2]

These differences are subtle, but I think they reveal a perspective shift that is starting to happen in Eve's heart. Perhaps perception deception is starting to sink in. Even though she doesn't fully agree with the serpent, it seems like the serpent's words are already at work, deceptively shifting her perspective. She's starting to see abundance as scarcity and blessing as affliction. Notice how the changes Eve made reveal a shifting perspective.

1. She deemphasizes the goodness of God's blessing – "Maybe God isn't that good."
2. She also deemphasizes the consequences – "Maybe eating isn't that bad."
3. She is shifting to a scarcity mindset by adding in additional prohibitions – "God won't let us do anything."

The shift always starts subtly, but it happens. Step by step, thought by thought. The serpent's words are having an effect. However, let's not get on our moral high horses and look down at Eve. We all do this. We all let deceptive voices shift our perspective from God's abundance to the lie of scarcity. Each of us takes small step after small step away from God's blessing and begins to feel like we're facing affliction. We often don't notice it because we rationalize the shift in small, subtle ways.

Notice how the serpent responds to Eve's statement. He's caught the subtle differences in what Eve said, so he goes in for the kill. He tries to convince her God cannot be trusted.

"You will not certainly die," the serpent said to the woman.

The serpent tells the woman, God is lying to you! The serpent then goes on to fan the flames of scarcity by insinuating God is holding out.

"For God knows that when you eat from it your eyes will be opened, and you will be like God, knowing good and evil."

The serpent's deception is targeted right at Eve's trust in God. When perception deception fully takes hold, the giver is now seen as the one withholding blessing. Trust begins to erode.

Remember the discovery we made as we looked at Genesis 1 & 2? God desires a relationship with his image-bearing partners that is grounded in a trust-filled intimate community. It's hard to have a relationship without trust. I think that's the crafty serpent's attack plan. If you can erode trust, you sabotage the relationship.

Allow me to jump ahead a couple of thousand years to Jesus. In the gospels, Jesus talks a lot about faith. He's impressed with outsiders who display more faith than insiders.[3] He says even a tiny bit of faith — mustard seed-sized faith — can still accomplish great things.[4] In other parts of the New Testament, Paul talks about how we are made right with God through faith.[5] The writer of Hebrews tells us how our faith pleases God. [6] Why all this talk about faith? Faith is another word for trust. Faith is not just an intellectual assertion or an item you possess. It is relational trust. Marcus Warner, president of Deeper Walk International, describes faith this way, "It is a bond with God that says, 'I trust you more than I trust what I can see and understand for myself.'"[7] Faith is trust that God is true to his character. Faith is trust that Jesus is who he said he was and does what he said he would do. Faith is trust that God really loves you and desires a relationship with you. Faith is about relational trust, and as we discussed in earlier chapters, trust is what God desires as the basis of his relationship with humanity — an intimate, trust-filled community.

In 1859, a French acrobat with the stage name Charles Blondin strung a rope across Niagara Falls and stunned audiences as he tightrope walked over the churning water. He performed this stunt many more times, increasing the spectacle with each crossing. He walked blindfolded, pushed a wheelbarrow, somersaulted, and backflipped; he even carried a small stove and cooked an omelet in the middle of the rope. Blondin successfully completed the walk dozens of times. All the while, his manager, Harry Colcord, watched and cheered with the crowd. I'm sure he believed that Blondin would complete each attempt. But then, Blondin asked his manager to get on his back so he could carry him piggyback across the falls. It's one thing to believe Blondin can cross with no problem. It's a whole different proposition to trust him to carry you! That's what the Bible talks about when it talks about faith. Faith is trusting yourself to God. It's more than knowing about God. It's putting your full weight into the relationship. Blondin's manager jumped on his back, and they successfully crossed the falls. I find Blondin's instructions to his manager so revealing as to what trust looks like.

> "You are no longer Colcord. You are Blondin. Until I clear this place, be a part of me, mind, body, and soul. If I sway, sway with me. Do not attempt to do any balancing yourself. If you do, we will both go to our death."[8]

That's the kind of trust God desires. We are invited to trust God with all our hearts, all our minds, and all our strength. When we do trust, we realize it's not up to us to keep our balance on the rope. We simply hold on and watch what God can do.

The reality is that kind of trust is difficult. I don't know about you, but I like to be in control. My family has one of those two-seat tandem bicycles. The back seat handlebars are fused to the front seat, but that doesn't stop me from trying to turn them when I'm in the back. I like to be in control, yet I've had to come to the difficult truth that there is very little I can control. The vast majority of my life and your life is built on trust. I have to trust my alarm will go off to wake me up. I have to trust the other drivers will stay in their lane on my commute to work. I have to trust my coworkers will complete their part of the project. That's not even getting into the deep trust required in marriage or in close friendships. Trust is key to any relationship, including with God, but that doesn't mean trust is easy. There are voices actively working to damage our trust in God. If the serpent's goal was to erode Eve's trust that God is good and his word is true, could it be possible that we could fall into the same trap? Perhaps Eve isn't the only one whose trust in God is in the crosshairs. If trust and faith in Christ are the lifeblood of every one of our relationships with God, it might be wise for us to pay attention to the serpent's tactics. How might our view of God be askew as a result of perception deception? As life doesn't turn out as we anticipate, we can begin to believe God is holding out on us. Or we might believe God is actively punishing us. Suddenly, his words don't hold as much weight in our minds. That's when we begin trusting other voices instead of God's.

So, how do we keep this from happening?
How do we not fall victim to the serpent's tactics?

It's beneficial to remind ourselves of how the story began. We fight perception deception by clinging to the truths we learn of God's character in the opening chapters of Genesis. It's a story of God's goodness, abundance, and blessing. It's a story of partnership and intimate community. It's a story showing God fully accepts and embraces his creation. It's a story worth trusting. We must learn to "trust the story."[9] God's character doesn't change. We'll dig into the truths about God's character revealed in the garden story in the second half of this book. But this is another reminder that the good news of the gospel starts with the truths of Genesis 1 and 2. God is trustworthy.

Back to Eve. The subtle changes she makes as she replies to the serpent, reveal her trust in God is at risk. But the process doesn't end here. Distrust, rooted in deception, is then fueled by desire.

CHAPTER 5

DESIRE

The woman saw that the fruit of the tree was good for food and pleasing to the eye, and also desirable for gaining wisdom... (GENESIS 3:6a)

The Marshmallow Test is one of the more famous pieces of social science research. The study was done to test the impact a variety of circumstances had on the ability of preschool-age children to delay gratification. The base experiment had an interesting premise. A child was brought into a room with only a table with a marshmallow on it. They were given the choice to eat the one marshmallow whenever they wanted, or if they could wait until the instructor returned, they would be rewarded with two marshmallows. Then, they were left alone for 15 minutes. That had to feel like an eternity for those kids! A variation of the study caught my attention. Before the marshmallows were brought out, the kids had one of two interactions with the researcher. For one group, the researcher made a promise and followed through on it. For the other group, the researcher made a promise and didn't follow through. They were essentially creating an atmosphere of trust or distrust with the researcher before the marshmallow was brought out. The group of kids who had a distrustful researcher waited, on average, three minutes and two seconds before eating the marshmallow. The kids who had a trustful researcher waited an average of twelve minutes and two seconds.[1] The kids that distrusted the researcher grabbed the marshmallows much sooner.

The same effect seems to be at play in the Garden of Eden. Perception deception has shifted Eve's perspective about God, and her trust is falling. Now, her desires come into play. She desires the thing God said was not good. Notice that this is the first time in the story someone other than God is defining what is good. Up to this point, any declaration of something being good or not good has come only from God. But now, with trust eroded, Eve begins to define good on her own terms. Notice that Eve "saw" that the fruit was "good." These are the same words God used to define good in Genesis 1, "God saw that it was good." Eve's statement is a contrasting parallel to how God saw all that he had made was good. Eve declares on her own that something is good.

But how does she determine her definition of good and evil?

It appears to be based on her desires. She saw the fruit was good for food and pleasing to the eye, and she desired it.

Remember what we concluded about the Tree of Knowledge of Good and Evil earlier? One of the main functions of the tree was to allow mankind to trust God's definition of good and evil. But when deception leads to distrust, our relationship with God struggles. If we fail to trust God, we're less likely to trust his definition of good and evil. We're then left to define what is good and what is evil in our own eyes. Our desire then reinforces the deception we've bought into. If I desire it, it must be good. If I dislike it, it must be evil.

Set a plate of chocolate and a plate of Brussels sprouts in front of a kid and ask them which is good and which is bad. The average kid will answer based on what they desire — what tastes good to them. Ask their parents which plate their child should eat for dinner, and you'll probably get a different answer. Why? Because parents desire something different for their child. They desire the health and flourishing of their children. They know that chocolate for dinner is not good. It will eventually lead to unhealth. Brussels sprouts are good because of the nutrients they carry. Part of a parent's job is to help their child learn what will lead to their flourishing, even if it isn't the thing they desire the most.

Similar dynamics are at play in the garden and in each of our hearts today. Without trust in God, we base our actions not on God's life-giving wisdom but on what looks good and pleasing to our own eyes. Just like the kid desiring chocolate for dinner, letting our desires control us will give momentary satisfaction but will rarely lead to health and flourishing. Let's be honest. This is part of the challenge facing our world today. Billions of people define good and evil based on their own desires. But what I desire may not be what you desire. In fact, it may be totally contrary. These competing desires lead to conflict externally and wreak havoc on the world God created. At the same time, we can have competing desires within ourselves. For example, I desire to be healthy, so I should exercise, but I also desire to sit on the couch watching Netflix and have a bowl of ice cream. These competing desires create conflict internally as well. Each of us has many desires pulling us and pushing us. Where do these desires come from, and why do they so often create problems for us?

I think it's time to come back to a question we brought up in chapter 3. What's the deal with the serpent that talks? If you've grown up in the church, you might not give this much thought. Perhaps you immediately assume the serpent is Satan and don't take time to think about how odd a talking snake is. That's not a wrong assumption. New Testament writers do connect the devil with serpent imagery.[2] But don't move past the serpent too quickly. There may be more going on than you realize. Remember earlier, I said this story is one of many Bible stories that is a casualty of the lullaby effect. We've heard the story so many times that we fail to see how strange it is. Why a snake that talks? To answer this, let's go back to the creation story in Genesis 1.

On the sixth day of creation, God made a distinction between humans and other living creatures. Humanity was created in the image of God. Other animals were not. God speaks uniquely and specifically to mankind as his image-bearing partners, instructing them to rule over the animals he created. Remember how we talked about the connection between image and rule?

> "God blessed them and said to them, "Be fruitful and increase in number; fill the earth and subdue it. Rule over the fish in the sea and the birds in the sky and over every living creature that moves on the ground." (GENESIS 1:28)

This is partnership language. Humanity is called to reflect God's authority, goodness, and order to the rest of creation as they rule over the other living creatures. You could think of it like this:

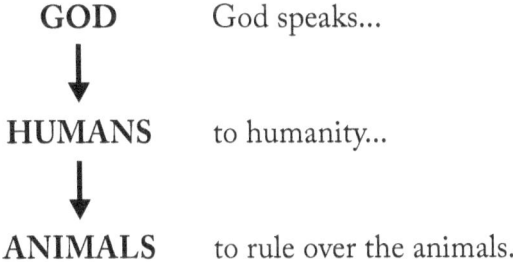

GOD   God speaks...

↓

HUMANS   to humanity...

↓

ANIMALS to rule over the animals.

But in Genesis 3, this talking serpent randomly appears in the story. A serpent is an animal. What does this animal do? It questions God's words, "Did God really say...?" So this is an animal... speaking to humans... questioning God's goodness and authority. The serpent completely subverts the order that God intended.

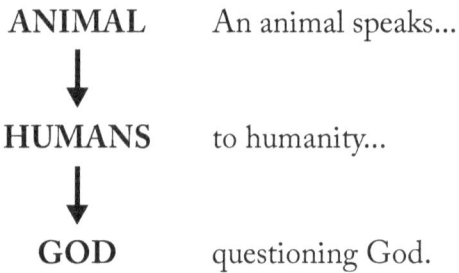

ANIMAL   An animal speaks...

HUMANS   to humanity...

GOD   questioning God.

Let's talk for a moment about animals and humans.

How do animals decide what to do?

Animals are driven by instinct — by their desires. That's how God created them. When an animal is hungry, it eats. When an animal is scared, it attacks. When it wants to mate, it mates. It is driven by its desires.

How do humans decide what to do?

In Genesis 1 & 2, humans are called to trust in God's words — what God has declared to be good and bad. In the creation accounts, man and woman are the only created beings that God speaks to. He blesses them. He instructs them on their role as partners, and he warns them of potential danger. What God says is meant to guide humanity on how to live in this intimate, trust-filled partnership. The relationship between God and humanity is to be built on trusting what God says.

The serpent, however, subverts this order and deceptively casts God as one not to be trusted. The tactic of the serpent is to get Eve to not trust God's word and instead to trust her own desires. In other words, the serpent wants Eve to be less human and more like an animal.

This garden story is creating a word picture of what it means to live in a trusting relationship with God's words (human) and what it means to live apart from that (animal). To be driven by our animal-like desires is to be less than what God created us to be.[3]

This battle between trusting God or our animalistic desires ripples through the rest of scripture. We see it in the next generation after Adam and Eve. God warns Cain that "sin is crouching at your door; it desires to have you, but you must rule over it."[4] Notice that sin is described in animal-like terms, crouching and desiring. God is reminding Cain that humanity's role is to rule over the animal, not be ruled by it. Five generations after Cain, we encounter the story of Lamech. Lamech brags to his wives, "I have killed a man for wounding me, a young man for injuring me."[5]

Lamech portrays an animalistic vengeance. You bite me; I bite back harder. These chapters in Genesis depict humanity moving further and further away from God's intended design and role — more animal-like and less human.

We see this same theme in the New Testament, especially in Paul's letters. Paul describes the animal and human tension with the language of Spirit and flesh. The Greek word translated as flesh carries the connotation of "the animal nature with cravings to incite sin."[6] Paul uses animal-like language to describe living according to the flesh, "If you bite and devour each other, watch out or you will be destroyed by each other."[7] I think Paul is playing off this Genesis idea. Living according to our fleshly desires is living less than human and more like an animal. In contrast, living by the Spirit is to be fully human. Spirit-led living accomplishes the original intent of the Garden of Eden — an intimate, trust-filled relationship. In the letter to the Galatians, Paul lays out a choice: trust your flesh or trust God's spirit in you. You choose.

> So I say, walk by the Spirit, and you will not gratify the desires of the flesh. For the flesh desires what is contrary to the Spirit, and the Spirit what is contrary to the flesh. They are in conflict with each other, so you are not to do whatever you want.
> (GALATIANS 5:16-17)

When I was in elementary, I loved reading the "Choose Your Own Adventure" books. The storyline of these books would come to a decision point, and the reader could choose. "If you choose to enter the cave, turn to page 31. If you choose to take the mountain trail, turn to page 53." One choice would lead to danger, the other to safety.

But I have to confess. I cheated when I read those books. I would flip ahead to see the outcomes on both pages, so I knew which one to pick.

Here in Galatians, Paul "flips ahead" for us and makes known the outcome of the choice between the flesh and the Spirit. He talks about what each choice produces or its fruit. Living by the flesh — our animal-like desires — produces things like hatred, jealousy, fits of rage, selfish ambition, dissensions, factions, and envy.[8] These are all things that destroy relationships and create pain. Just like a child choosing chocolate every night for dinner, if we're driven by our desires, we will become unhealthy relationally and spiritually. But if we choose to trust God and let his spirit guide us, it produces something different. Its fruit is love, joy, peace, patience, kindness, goodness, faithfulness, gentleness, and self-control.[9] These are things that build up relationships and bring health and flourishing to life. God makes known the outcome of the choices we have between the flesh and the spirit. One leads to a life in tune with our created intent — fully human. The other leads to being less than what God intends — animal-like. The choice is ours.

But it's not always an easy choice, is it? Those desires are strong. Think back to the plates of chocolate and Brussels sprouts. Let's be honest. Most of us would desire the chocolate over Brussels sprouts as well. It's what we crave. But there's another deeper desire that might make us choose vegetables over candy — the desire to be healthy. One of the ways we battle animal-like desires is by letting the Spirit of God point us to deeper God-given desires.

Let me clarify something. The desires we feel aren't necessarily bad in themselves. God has given us desires. He created our bodies to hunger and thirst. He created our hearts to seek comfort and security. He gave us the desire for intimacy and connection. These desires are part of the goodness of creation. They're meant to point us back to God as a way to reinforce the intimate, trust-filled relationship. The problem is our flesh distorts those God-given desires into animal-like cravings. We look for the quickest, self-focused way to satisfy those desires. We choose candy instead of a well-balanced meal because the candy is quicker and easier. As the prophet Isaiah reveals, our God-given desires are meant to lead us to him, yet we often choose things that don't satisfy us.

> Come, all you who are thirsty,
>   come to the waters;
> and you who have no money,
>   come, buy, and eat!
> Come, buy wine and milk

> without money and without cost.
> Why spend money on what is not bread
>   and your labor on what does not satisfy?
> Listen, listen to me, and eat what is good,
>   and you will delight in the richest of fare.
> Give ear and come to me;
>   listen, that you may live.
> (ISAIAH 55:1-3)

So, what do we do with the desires we have? Often, we approach them in one of two ways. We either give in or try to suppress and ignore them. But if these desires are God-given, instead of giving in or ignoring them, what if you get curious about your desires? What if you trust the Spirit of God inside you to help lead you to the deeper God-given desire that may be distorted? Remember, the fruit of the Spirit is self-control. You don't have to immediately say yes to that craving. What if, instead, you paused and got curious about why you desire what you desire? What could be underneath it? Could your desire for lust really be a deeper desire for intimacy and connection? Could the reason you binge another episode on Netflix be because you desire to be part of a bigger story, and there is something about your current life that isn't fulfilling? Could the reason you grab another drink or take another hit be because you want to numb the pain you're feeling? What if God could bring healing to that pain? Trust that God is good. He is the one who can truly fulfill and truly satisfy our deepest desires. God has given us desires to drive us towards him.

Our flesh can distort desires, but we can trust the Spirit of God to restore the desires God has given our hearts.

> Trust in the Lord and do good;
>> dwell in the land and enjoy safe pasture.
> Take delight in the Lord,
>> and he will give you the desires of your heart.
> Commit your way to the Lord;
>> trust in him, and he will do this.
> (PSALM 37:3-5)

Did you notice the "trust sandwich" of this Psalm? Before and after the verse about God giving the desires of our heart are two strong encouragements about trust and relationship. Desire is meant to be connected to our trust in God. Trust is the foundation. Our desires are to lead us to God, and then those same desires are transformed in the presence of his love.

The trust-filled intimate relationship with God is made possible through the Holy Spirit inside every follower of Christ. The journey of faith is to learn to trust the still small voice of the Spirit of God to lead us instead of our fleshly, animalistic desires. But ultimately, the choice is ours. We get to choose our own adventure.

Perhaps the biggest deception of the serpent is to get us to think the "truest" version of ourselves can be found in our base instincts apart from trust in God's word. But there's good news. You and I were created for more. Our desires don't have to dictate our direction. We can be truly human. We can choose trust.

But sometimes, that desire is too strong, and the fruit looks too good, so we reach out and take it.

CHAPTER 6

DISOBEDIENCE

"...she took some and ate it. She also gave some
to her husband, who was with her, and he ate it."
(GENESIS 3:6b)

When I was a kid, I was given a BB gun as a birthday gift.
My dad taught me how to use it safely and how to aim and
shoot. He taught me that I not only needed to be aware of
my target, but I needed to be aware of what was around
the target because if I missed, I could damage something I
didn't intend to. My dad watched over the first several times
I shot the BB gun. I got pretty good at lining up my shot
and hitting the empty cans we'd lined up on our makeshift
shooting range. There was something satisfying hearing that
"plink" and knowing the BB hit its target. When my dad felt
I was able to be trusted, he let me shoot unsupervised. He

left me with this warning, "Brent, I want you to only shoot at cans. Don't shoot at any animals. If you kill something, you have to eat it." I think my dad knew the temptation a BB gun in young hands might cause. He wanted to instill in me a respect for the life of other things; we don't indiscriminately kill. If you hunt an animal, there needs to be a purpose to it. I agreed to his terms and was out on my own, BB gun in hand.

Well, a little boy can only shoot cans for so long before they lose their allure. So, I went walking around the yard in search of other targets. As I came around the front yard, I looked up and saw a row of birds perched on the power lines. They were lined up like sitting ducks (I mean like sitting starlings.) I loaded my BB gun, took aim, and pulled the trigger. There was no "plink," but one of the starlings fell to the ground and flopped around. My gut wrenched as I watched this bird take its last breath. My dad must have seen me hunched over this dead bird with my rifle in hand because he came out the front door carrying a skillet! "Do you remember what I said?" he asked me. Thankfully, I didn't have to eat that bird. I think my dad realized I learned a lesson.

I had hit *my* target. But at the same time, I completely missed another target.

The Bible has several ways it describes sin. In the New Testament, the Greek word for sin carries the connotation of "missing the target."[1] It is the metaphorical idea of an archer missing the intended target. Just as my dad tried to teach me: if we miss the target, we can cause real damage.

The moment Eve and Adam eat the fruit, they disobey God's command. They sin. In the New Testament, Paul would describe this as the moment "sin entered the world."[2] It's often referred to as the Fall of Man. If this is the problem that the gospel is the solution for, we should take some time to understand what is going on in light of this garden narrative. So, let's talk about sin.

WHAT'S THE TARGET?

If sin is missing the target, the question that follows is, what is the target? Is the target a list of rules? Is the target perfect obedience? Sometimes, the aim of the Christian life can be presented as keeping some sort of impersonal moral standard. Sin is presented as the list of things we aren't allowed to do, and God is the cosmic rule keeper watching out. We can get the idea that sin is just my failure to keep the rules that God made up.

But the garden story presents a different picture. We see that God didn't create humanity to be perfectly obedient robotic servants. God desires an intimate trust-filled relationship where his image-bearing partners reflect his goodness into creation.

What if the target isn't rule-keeping but a personal relationship?

If the target is an intimate trust-filled community, then sin is anything that causes damage to our relationship with God and our relationship with others. Adam and Eve eating the fruit wasn't an isolated moment of rule-breaking. It was a breakdown of relationships — a failure to trust. In the church, we often talk about sin in legal terms — in terms of guilt and punishment. There is Biblical precedent for that, but at its core, sin is relationally missing the target. It's a failure to love and to trust God and others. So, instead of simply breaking a rule, sin is the fracturing of a relationship — with God and with others. That's why Jesus would teach the two greatest commandments are to love God and love your neighbor. Think back to little Brent with the BB gun. You could say I sinned because I broke a rule my dad set. But the target wasn't simply obedience to a rule. The target was my relationship with my dad and the way he desired I live in the world – to value the life of other things. When I missed the target, trust was the casualty.

The first few chapters of Genesis set the Biblical truth — it's all about relationships. It's all about how we interact with God and with others. What we define as the target matters because it impacts how we understand sin, salvation, and, ultimately, the Gospel.

SYMPTOMS

The moment that Adam and Eve ate from the fruit wasn't an isolated incident. It didn't happen on its own. Notice everything that led up to this moment. This act of disobedience didn't just randomly happen. It was a step in a process that started the moment the serpent's words shifted Eve's focus from abundance to scarcity. Here's the path we've identified so far…

Deception: The serpent shifts Eve's view from abundance to scarcity. Perception deception sets in.

Distrust: When perception deception fully takes hold, the giver is now seen as the one withholding blessing. Eve's trust in God begins to erode.

Desire: A lack of trust leads Eve away from letting God's words lead her and instead lets her desires lead her. Her desires become the new way she defines good and evil.

Disobedience: Eve and Adam act upon their desires and disobey God — sin.

Eve didn't just randomly sin one day. Her disobedience was the outcome of several other factors playing together. Perception Deception eroded her trust in God, allowing her desires to redefine good and bad. Her act of eating from the tree of the knowledge of good and evil happened because she chose to redefine good and evil in her own eyes.

We often present sin as *the* problem. Don't get me wrong, our sinful actions are a problem and cause much damage in the world, and we must take steps as followers of Jesus to turn away from sin. But when we focus on sin as *the* problem, we're only treating the symptoms of a deeper issue.

Recently, I heard a doctor share the story of a lady who, in her early 40s, had signs of dementia. The doctors she initially visited focused on her brain and tried to treat her neurologically. Those treatments didn't help, so she came to this doctor for a second opinion. He did some tests and discovered she had suffered multiple strokes due to untreated diabetes.[3] Dementia wasn't the problem; it was a symptom of untreated diabetes. She didn't have health insurance and couldn't access preventative treatments. That, in turn, caused a ripple effect of symptoms and complications. She only found full healing when the doctors in the public hospital treated the root cause and not the symptoms.

When we focus on sin as *the* problem, the solutions we provide focus on behavior modification. The Christian world is full of sermons and studies that focus on how to stop sinning. We come up with all kinds of elaborate ways to remove temptations, create boundaries, and develop accountability. Those aren't bad, but they only focus on the symptoms of the problem. The church world spends a lot of time, energy, and resources on programs that treat the symptoms. The unintended consequence of the "gospel of sin management" is shame. If churches only treat the symptom and not the problem, then people will always fall back to sin. They know they shouldn't. They've tried very hard not to. But their behavior hasn't changed because the deeper issues weren't addressed. That leaves many feeling defeated and weighed down with shame, thinking they are unworthy.

The garden story shows us that sin is the result of deeper things. Perhaps our view of God or our view of ourselves is distorted. Perhaps there are other voices we're listening to that deceive us. Perhaps that deception is causing us to blame God and erode our trust in him. Perhaps we're redefining what's good and what's evil based on our own desires instead of trusting God. Oswald Chambers wrote, "The root of all sin is the suspicion that God isn't good." This is exactly what we see perception deception lead to in the garden. Eve doubts God's goodness, and things begin to unravel.

The garden story reminds us that deeper than any type of sin management or behavior modification is the heart of God for relationships. There's a saying that "rules without relationship lead to rebellion."[4] I think that's what we see in the garden. The trust-filled relationship between God and humanity began to erode.

The error many good-hearted Christians make is they

approach God through the lens of obedience and punishment. The relational pursuit of God is stripped away from the gospel, and it's presented primarily as a legal transaction to avoid punishment in hell. As a result, evangelism is boiled down to a glorified sales pitch.

Step 1: Convince them they're a sinner.

Step 2: Tell them sin leads to eternal punishment in hell.

Step 3: Tell them if they accept Jesus, they can go to heaven instead of hell.

This presentation of the Gospel presents salvation as a transaction and is motivated by fear. Jesus becomes the ticket to get me away from something bad. It leads to bare minimum thinking, "what's the least I have to do to ensure I am saved?" It also has no power to truly change how someone lives.

But the story of the Bible, from the garden to the gospels, is that Jesus creates a way back to the beautiful trust-filled community we were originally created for. His life, death, and resurrection show us the extent to which God is willing to go to pursue us. Through Christ, we are able to redeem our role as God's partners in stewarding creation. We're not just saved to go to heaven. We're saved to partner with God to help accomplish his will "on earth as it is in heaven," or as my friend Joel says, "to bring the up there down here."[5] That's what requires trust and faith — to believe that God invites us to help bring the Kingdom of God in the midst of the kingdoms of our worlds. To be people who pursue love over power. To offer forgiveness instead of seeking vengeance. To live as if the first will be last and the last will be first. You can't live as a citizen of the Kingdom of God if your motivation is simply fear of punishment. There has to be more.

I remember an elementary teacher whose approach to classroom management was to have students make a mark on the board if they did something wrong. Too many marks and you'd go to the principal's office. If you did something good or helpful, you might be able to go up and erase one of your marks. You can debate whether that is a healthy approach to classroom management, but I sure felt the pressure when a mark was on the board and a relief when I got to erase a mark. But the motivation for my behavior was only about fearing punishment and desiring reward. An interesting thing would happen when a substitute teacher came in who didn't know about the marks on the board system. The class would go crazy. Our behavior was tied to the fear of punishment. Remove that, and all our behavior changed. The teachers I remember the most were the ones who did their best to build relationships with students. I knew they cared about me and wanted the best for me. That made me want to behave and do my best in their class. Behavior flowed out of the relationship.

If we see the story of scripture through the lens of fearing punishment, we miss the relational desire of God, and we miss the fullness of the gospel. What Jesus did provides more than just a "get out of jail free" card. He provides a way to restore our relationship. The gospel doesn't start in Genesis chapter 3. When we use Genesis 1-2 as the foundation, we see Adam and Eve's disobedience in a different light. It was a breach of relationship. Their sin was the symptom of a deeper problem. Sin is serious, yes. Not because we get a "mark on the board" and fear punishment, but because it damages relationships…as we will see.

CHAPTER 7

DIVISION

Then, the eyes of both of them were opened, and they realized they were naked, so they sewed fig leaves together and made coverings for themselves. Then the man and his wife heard the sound of the Lord God as he was walking in the garden in the cool of the day, and they hid from the Lord God among the trees of the garden. But the Lord God called to the man, "Where are you?" He answered, "I heard you in the garden, and I was afraid because I was naked; so I hid." And he said, "Who told you that you were naked? Have you eaten from the tree that I commanded you not to eat from?" The man said, "The woman you put here with me — she gave me some fruit from the tree, and I ate it." Then the Lord God said to the woman, "What is this you have done?" The woman said, "The serpent deceived me, and I ate." (GENESIS 3:7-13)

I was in elementary school when Reebok came out with their pump sneakers. They were the coolest shoes I had ever seen. You could squeeze a little basketball-styled pump on the tongue of the shoe and inflate air chambers inside for a custom fit. A kid in my class had a pair, and everyone wanted a turn to pump them up. I really wanted those shoes. The only problem was they were out of my family's price range. But, at the start of the next school year, when it was time to buy back-to-school shoes, I discovered that Franklin had created their own "knock-off" brand of pumps. These were in the right price range. I bought them, and for the next several days, I pumped and repumped those shoes. I swear they made me run faster and jump higher. The first day of school arrived, and I proudly wore my Franklin pump shoes, ready to show them off to everyone in my class. But my joy was quickly smothered. Some of the other kids began to make fun of my shoes. They made it clear to me through a variety of jokes and mean comments that my shoes were *not* Reeboks; they weren't real pumps. Now, I knew my shoes were not Reeboks when I bought them. But after that first day of school, I *knew* my shoes were not Reeboks.

Do you get what I'm saying?

After Adam and Eve eat the fruit, scripture says they realized they were naked, which is an interesting statement given the fact they were naked their whole existence up to that point. Did they not know? What changed? Perhaps this is like my experience with Reebok pumps. Their realization wasn't factual. It was experiential and wrapped in shame. I think Adam and Eve were aware of their nakedness before, but after eating the fruit, they *knew* they were naked. Something external had changed their internal perception. It's the full effect of perception deception. Something that was intended as a blessing is now an affliction. The shoes I once was proud of now brought shame. Adam and Eve were ashamed about their nakedness, which earlier held no shame. Isn't it interesting how quickly our perspectives can change?

In verse 7, the word translated as "realized" is the same Greek word translated as "to know" earlier in the story. Remember how we talked about the experiential nature of knowing? Adam and Eve don't just know about evil. They now *know* evil because they've experienced it.

Adam and Eve's eyes were "opened." Their innocence was lost. Now they have something to hide. They fear being fully known. As we discussed earlier, nakedness in this story isn't about physical nakedness. It's a metaphor for relational and emotional nakedness. God's original intent was to create a community of relational nakedness where there was nothing to hide. Everyone could fully be themselves and experience full acceptance. One of the things that makes sin so serious is the damage it inflicts on relationships. We see Adam and Eve's sin lead to division. The intimacy and openness between the two humans is fractured, and so they hide behind fig leaves.

Fig leaves haven't gone out of fashion, have they?

We all wear fig leaves to hide parts of ourselves from others. We all wear masks around certain people. We hide our flaws, failures, and fears and then try to portray an image we think will make us more acceptable to those around us. Social media has allowed us to present perfectly curated images of ourselves to the world. We hide the parts we'd rather not show and add filters to smooth out the rough edges. It also means when we look at other people's posts, we're not seeing reality, yet we judge ourselves against their seemingly perfect lives, families, or appearance. It just results in more shame. Our perfectly manicured social media posts are just modern fig leaves. It's a tactic as old as the garden. It occasionally fools other people. It never fools God.

Fig leaves reveal the damage done to relationships. God asks Adam and Eve, "Who told you that you were naked? Have you eaten from the tree that I commanded you not to eat from?" Notice how Adam responds. "The woman you put here with me — she gave me some fruit from the tree, and I ate it." Adam shifts the blame to God — YOU put her here with me! I didn't choose her! And he shifts the blame to Eve — SHE gave it to me! Again, perception deception is at work, causing blessing to be seen as affliction. Adam sees his God-given helper as a hindrance. How many relationships have fallen victim to this perspective shift?

There's a division between man and woman. There's also a

division between humans and God. God's original intent was an intimate, trust-filled community with humanity. But now we see that when Adam and Eve heard the sound of God walking in the garden, they hid from him. The Hebrew word that the NIV translates as "sound" also means "voice."[1] It was hearing God's voice that caused them to hide. This is interesting, considering the observation we made in earlier chapters that humans were the only ones in creation that God spoke to. God intended his voice to be a means toward an intimate, trust-filled relationship, but now, it's at the sound of God's voice that Adam and Eve hide.

Also, notice where they are hiding.

> "they hid from the Lord God among the trees of the garden."

The trees were a symbol of God's abundant blessing. Trees given as gifts to enjoy and eat are now the things used as a barrier to hide behind. We can see the distortion of what God intended as good being used to separate.

So, why are they hiding?

Adam says, "I heard you in the garden, and I was afraid because I was naked, so I hid." Adam hears God's voice and is afraid. Notice the shift in the relationship. The relationship that once was marked by intimacy, trust, and partnership is now marked by fear, shame, and hiding.

Fear divides humanity from God. We were never meant to relate to God on the basis of fear. John lays out this truth in his letter, "There is no fear in love. But perfect love drives out fear, because fear has to do with punishment. The one who fears is not made perfect in love."[2]

The other day, as I was driving, I glanced in the rearview mirror and noticed a cop car following me. Suddenly, a low-grade fear and anxiety swept over me, just waiting for the moment the cop would turn on his lights. I was obeying traffic laws before I noticed the cop following me, but I did so fearfully when I realized the cop was behind me. The cop car eventually turned, and I breathed a sigh of relief. I think many of us view God in the same way. He's on patrol, just waiting for us to screw up so he can turn on his lights and give us a ticket.

I've had many conversations with people who have an under-lying fear that characterizes their relationship with God. For some, the motivation for choosing God was the fear of hell. Others miss God's grace and operate out of a relationship that looks more like karma — when they do good, they'll be blessed, and when they do bad, they'll be punished. I've talked to others who do what pastors like me tell them — to read their Bibles — but they read everything through the lens of fear, and God's promises are distorted into curses. Again, perception deception at work — what is meant to be a blessing is instead seen as a curse. But we were never meant to relate to God based on fear. The opening pages of Genesis show us a God who desires intimacy and trust. Fear erodes both of those things and creates division in relationships. Relationships bonded in fear don't thrive. God's intent is to let love be the strong bond to let relationships flourish. Fear separates us relationally, while love connects us deeper with others. Fear is about avoidance, while love is about attraction.[3]

The challenging thing about fear and love is they can produce similar outward expressions. It can be difficult to know where the core motivation comes from. Let's look at generosity, for example. I can do something generous because I'm motivated by God's generosity towards me. In other words, my generous actions flow out of the love I feel from God. However, I can also do the same generous act because I'm afraid God will punish me if I don't. Fear is the motivation here. The action looks the same on the outside, but the internal motivations couldn't be further apart. The difference between these two motivations impacts relationships.

It's not just the religious world that understands the negative impact of fear. Business researchers have found the negative impact fear has on a workplace culture. Business consultant Kathleen Ryan shares in her book *"Driving Fear Out of the Workplace"* that fear doesn't motivate toward constructive action. On the contrary, it nourishes competition within an organization, fosters short-term thinking, destroys trust, erodes joy and pride in work, stifles innovation, and distorts communication."[4] Fear "destroys trust" and "distorts communication." That sounds a lot like what we've seen in the garden story, doesn't it?

The division we see between Adam and Eve is rooted in the fear of rejection. They fear being "naked" with each other because they fear their whole true selves won't be accepted. The same is true of our relationship with God. We can fear rejection, punishment, and condemnation. Too often, the messages we receive about God reinforce those distorted perceptions. When we let these fear-based messages take hold, our relationships suffer just like Adam and Eve's.

Adam and Eve's distorted perceptions of God led to a breakdown of the relationship and a lack of trust, resulting in fear. This fear creates a division between man and woman and a division between humanity and God. That division comes at a cost. If God is the source of life, then what happens when humanity is separated from him?

CHAPTER 8

DEATH

"...for when you eat from it you will certainly die."
(GENESIS 2:17b)
"You will not certainly die," the serpent said to the
woman." (GENESIS 3:4)
"So the LORD God banished him from the Garden of
Eden..." (GENESIS 3:23)

At every funeral I've officiated, there is an interesting mix
of emotions present. There's a sense of profound loss. There's
a feeling of comfort and support from family and friends.
There are even humorous moments as loved ones share
stories of the deceased. But underneath all those feelings is
a slightly unsettling discomfort. Coming face to face with
death is uncomfortable. I'm sure some of that is due to our
modern American culture that tends to ignore mortality,
but the truth of the garden shows we were never meant to

experience death. We weren't created for it. We should be uncomfortable with it. Every experience with death is a reminder of what should be, that we were designed for life. There is a longing for the garden in all of us, whether we realize it or not.

Let's address an interesting tension in scripture. When God warns Adam and Eve about the outcome of eating the fruit, it almost seems like death would be an immediate outcome. At least, that's the impression I get. Perhaps I've seen too many movies where characters are poisoned and immediately drop dead, just like "*The Princess Bride.*" But Adam and Eve don't immediately drop dead. Now, astute readers will point out that Adam and Eve do eventually die. Genesis 5:5 says, "Altogether, Adam lived a total of 930 years, and then he died." So yes, what God said is true, even though it took nearly a millennium to happen. But if we only focus on that fact, I think we miss some of what the story is trying to get us to understand. Experiencing death isn't just about the cessation of life. Adam and Eve may not have immediately died, but they aren't fully living either.

Even if their death wasn't immediate, death's effects were imminent. Death can still be experienced before we breathe our last breath. Adam and Eve experienced death on multiple levels. They experienced the death of God's intended design for creation. They experienced the death of intimacy and trust with the creator. They lived the rest of their days with the longing for the garden, acutely aware that their current experience wasn't what it should be. They experienced the death of a child. In the very next story, out of the garden, one of their sons brutally kills the other. Adam and Eve knew God's warning to be true even before their hearts stopped beating.

Some people interpret death as a punishment for Adam and Eve's disobedience. In my opinion, this story presents death not as a direct punishment but as the tragic yet logical result of Adam and Eve's choices. We see from the very beginning that God is the source of life. He breathes life into humanity. The garden story symbolizes the connection to divine life as a tree — the tree of life. To be fully alive is to be connected to God. In the same way, for a light bulb to shine, it must be plugged in. Adam and Eve's choices have impacted their relationship with the giver of life. As their trust erodes, Adam and Eve's actions lead them out of the garden. They are no longer in intimate connection to this divine life. The result is death — relationally and physically. A death they experience in many real and tangible ways before their mortal lives end. This is the ultimate tragedy of the path we've seen unfolding. An outcome that God never intended.

Sometimes, the church can focus so much on what happens after you die that we fail to address the death you're currently experiencing all around you. Many things beyond our control can feel like death: a job loss, the end of a relationship, or a health issue that interferes with your plans. The question is, what do you do with these losses?

The entire world felt a loss during 2020 and the Covid-19 pandemic. Grief was everywhere, it seemed. So many people lost loved ones to the virus. Several lost their health due to complications of "long COVID." Relationships suffered as people were locked down. Businesses struggled. We all lost our sense of normalcy and daily routine. Those circumstances, combined with some ministry struggles, left me in a daze. It was in this season that I discovered the gift of lament.

Lament is a form of prayer where you cry out to God, grieving all that shouldn't be. While pain, suffering, and grief can often push us away from faith, lament is an intentional practice of bringing all those feelings to God. We choose to talk to God rather than about God. Lament acknowledges that what is going on is not what God intends for his creation. It's a way to work through the grieving process. On the surface, it may sound like lament is just bringing complaints to God, but it's really about discovering trust.

The book of Psalms is a collection of songs and poems that marked the worship of ancient Jews and many of us today. In general, there are three types of psalms: psalms of praise, psalms of thanksgiving, and psalms of lament. Interestingly, there are more psalms of lament than any other type of psalm. Psalms of lament don't get put on coffee mugs or hung on the wall, but they clearly provided ancient Jews with a powerful way to connect with God.

Psalm 13 is a psalm of lament. Notice the raw language the psalmist uses to express grief and frustration to God. Notice also what expressing those feelings leads to at the end of the psalm.

> How long, LORD? Will you forget me forever?
>   How long will you hide your face from me?
> How long must I wrestle with my thoughts
>   and day after day have sorrow in my heart?
>   How long will my enemy triumph over me?
> Look on me and answer, LORD my God.
>   Give light to my eyes, or I will sleep in death,
> and my enemy will say, "I have overcome him,"
>   and my foes will rejoice when I fall.
> But I trust in your unfailing love;
>   my heart rejoices in your salvation.
> I will sing the LORD's praise,
>   for he has been good to me.

Lament is an act of trust. Through lament we acknowledge that we have a heavenly father who cares how we feel and is concerned with what we're going through. He is a father to whom we can express our frustrations, desires, and unmet expectations. I found that as I brought laments to God, I discovered an underlying hope that began to quiet my cynicism. It didn't change the circumstances or remove grief, but it helped me see that God was worth trusting and was with me in the midst of it all. Even in the midst of death, God is present.

The choice to trust God — with grief, with our futures, and more — sets the trajectory of how we experience the world. The ultimate goal of this book is to help you see that God is worth trusting. However, we've spent the first half of the book trying to understand how trust is lost. The Garden of Eden story sheds light on that. Let's remind ourselves of the path we've discovered that leads to the fall of trust.

Abundance and Blessing: The story starts with God creating humanity as his partner in an intimate, trust-filled relationship. God blesses them abundantly with all the trees in the garden and warns them about one.

Deception: The serpent shifts Eve's view from abundance to scarcity. Perception Deception sets in.

Distrust: When perception deception fully takes hold, the giver is now seen as the one withholding blessing. Trust begins to erode.

Desire: A lack of trust leads Eve away from letting God's words lead her and instead lets her desires lead her. Her desires become the new way she defines good and evil.

Disobedience: Eve and Adam act upon their desires and disobey God.

Division: Eve and Adam's actions create division between each other and between them and God. Instead of an intimate, trust-filled relationship, there is now fear, shame, and hiding.

Death: Separation from the life-giving God ultimately leads to death — physically and relationally.[1]

Hopefully, you're beginning to see that the story of the garden isn't just about two people at the beginning of creation. It's about every one of us. It's the story of how we all can be deceived, how we all can struggle to trust God, how we all can choose to follow our own desires instead of living in step with our creator, and how we all experience death before we actually die. Genesis 3 isn't just a story about how "sin entered the world." It's a story that illuminates each of our hearts to reveal why we choose to disobey, separate ourselves from God, and experience the resulting fallout in our lives. When we fail to trust God and follow our own animal-like desires, things begin to wither and die. We turn inward. Relationships suffer. Hearts harden. Fear, shame, and condemnation mark our connection with the divine. Hope, joy, and wonder can slowly die.

Let's be honest. This is all a little depressing, isn't it?

Hang in there. The good news is we're not done making discoveries. This may be the end of part one of this book, but it's far from the end of the garden story. There's more buried treasure to dig up. In part two, we'll discover that while humanity struggles to trust God, God never loses trust in us. Even in the midst of disobedience, division, and death, there are glimpses of God's faithfulness. He isn't going to let the story die. Woven into this text are truths about God's character and his promises. You see, God has a way of bringing dead things back to life.

PART TWO

THE TRUST IN THE FALL

CHAPTER 9

THAT, AND MORE

In the spring of 1998, the band Semisonic released a song on their second album that has been played as the last song of the night in bars across the country. The lyrics of "Closing Time" just fit the scenario too well. If you're not familiar with late 90s alternative rock (or, as my son says, "that lame 90s music you listen to"), here are some of the lyrics...

> Closing time, open all the doors
> And let you out into the world
> Closing time, turn all of the lights on
> Over every boy and every girl
>
> Closing time, one last call for alcohol
> So, finish your whiskey or beer
> Closing time, you don't have to go home
> But you can't stay here.

I know who I want to take me home
I know who I want to take me home
I know who I want to take me home

Closing time, time for you to go out
To the places you will be from
Closing time, this room won't be open
Till your brothers or your sisters come

So, gather up your jackets, move them to the exits
I hope you have found a friend
Closing time, every new beginning
Comes from some other beginning's end

See what I mean? It's the perfect song for a bar to send its patrons happily out into the night so it can close. It's also the song Semisonic would close out their concerts with.

But the song is not just about leaving a bar or ending a concert. It's actually about birth! The lead singer's wife was pregnant with their first child as he was writing this song. The lyrics express the transition of birth and the new beginnings it represents.[1]

With this new lens, read through the lyrics again. They hit a little differently, don't they?
"Turn all of the lights on over every boy and every girl."
"Time for you to go out to the places you will be from."

"This room won't be open till your brothers or your sisters come."

How did I miss this all the times I sang the song at the top of my lungs in the late 90s?

Isn't it interesting how you can see something the same way for so long, then suddenly see it in a different way? This new perspective doesn't necessarily negate the previous one. Seeing the song in this new light doesn't mean bars can't play it anymore. The beauty of art is that it speaks on multiple levels. The song can be about leaving a bar as it closes. It can also be about that and more. I find the "and more" part to be where things get interesting.

The same is true of the Bible. You can see something the same way for years, then suddenly discover a deeper perspective. I think that's what the writer of Hebrews was getting at by describing the word of God as "alive and active."[2]

We've journeyed through the Fall of Man in Genesis 3. We discovered how perception deception can lead to distrust and the breakdown of the intimate, trust-filled relationship God desires. We discovered how the garden story isn't just an account of how sin entered the world, but it reveals how all of us struggle to trust God today. The majority of the time I hear Genesis 3 referenced in the church, it's to talk about the failure of humanity. Sure, it's about that, but it's also about more. It reveals truths about ourselves, and more importantly, it reveals truths about God's character. I've discovered that this garden story isn't just about what went wrong. It is a foundational look into the goodness, grace, and patient love of our creator. It sets the foundation for how we should read and interpret the rest of the Biblical story.

In the same way you'll experience "Closing Time" in a different way the next time you hear it, I hope that the second half of this book will help you see the garden story in a new way. There is so much left to discover.

CHAPTER 10

HIDE AND SEEK

Then the man and his wife heard the sound of the LORD God as he was walking in the garden in the cool of the day, and they hid from the LORD God among the trees of the garden. But the LORD God called to the man, "Where are you?"
He answered, "I heard you in the garden, and I was afraid because I was naked; so I hid."
(GENESIS 3:8-10)

The greatest game of hide and seek I ever played happened when I was in sixth grade. It was a Halloween party at my friend's house, and about 20 of my fellow middle school students joined in. It was a crisp fall night with no moon, which made hiding a little easier. I happened to be wearing all-dark clothing, which was a serendipitous plus. After a few rounds, I spied a tall pine tree in the corner of my friend's yard, and I quickly climbed nearly to the top. I hung on as silently as I could. A moment later, someone else had the same idea and climbed halfway up the tree. I didn't say a word. They didn't know I was above them. Then, a third person came and lay on the ground below the pine tree, unaware two other people were above. The seeker cried out, "Ready or not, here I come," and began the search. I watched from my perch as the seeker looked all over the yard, finding person after person. It wasn't too long before the person on the ground under the tree was discovered. A little while later, the person below me was found. Eventually, everyone else had been found. I was the last one left! I couldn't wait to revel in the glory of being the ultimate hider. But a funny thing happened. Everyone stopped looking for me and went inside for snacks. I was left alone hiding, with my only reward being tree sap in my hair. Are you really hiding if no one is looking for you?

The first ever game of hide and seek was in the Garden of Eden after Adam and Eve disobeyed God. In chapter seven, we saw that Adam and Eve hid because of fear and shame. Adam heard the voice of God and hid because he was afraid. If we place all our focus on Adam and Eve's actions, we can miss this truth: God was seeking them out.

The text doesn't specify, but I think it's a safe assumption that God knew what Adam and Eve had done. God knew where they were hiding when he called out, "Where are you?" It's one of those questions loaded with meaning. God was acknowledging things weren't right in the relationship. But with that question, he's also acknowledging he hasn't abandoned Adam and Eve either. He's seeking them out. God knows about their disobedience, yet he's still seeking them out.

After Adam responds, God asks another question loaded with meaning. "Who told you that you were naked?" In other words, "What other voice are you listening to?" Remember, God used his voice to speak specifically to Adam and Eve, unique to all creation. He desired his voice to be the guide leading them toward wisdom and flourishing. With this simple question, God is reminding Adam and Eve of his desire that they trust his voice. But notice this: not only is God still seeking, but he's also still speaking.

Don't miss this. Adam and Eve have failed to trust God. They have sinned and missed the mark. Humanity has fallen. God's good creation is fractured. Yet God is still seeking and speaking. He isn't repulsed by their actions. God doesn't vanish from their presence. God doesn't step back and wait for Adam and Eve to apologize or change. God is actively pursuing Adam and Eve. He is seeking and speaking.

I often hear and use the phrase "sin separates us from God." I believe that phrase to be true, but sometimes I think we can understand it in the wrong way. Sometimes, we understand it to mean God pulls away from us because we're sinful. I can't tell you the number of conversations I've had with people who when I invite them to join me at church, joke about how God will send a lightning bolt to burn them up if they enter the church. Underneath their lighthearted refusal is an assumption that God wants nothing to do with them until they "change their ways." My friend, who works with people in the recovery community, shared about how those in the midst of active addiction feel like God wants nothing to do with them. Maybe you've felt that way too. Maybe you think your mistakes have disqualified you from God. Is this how God operates? Not according to the garden story. Who separates themselves from whom?

Who are the ones hiding?

It's not God that pulls away. Adam and Eve, driven by their shame and fear, pull away from God. Yes, sin separates us from God, but it's because we hide from God. God never pulls away from us. He never stops seeking.

The larger narrative of scripture is the process of God seeking to dwell more intimately with humanity. In Exodus, we see God give specific instructions for his people to build a tabernacle, a giant portable tent, that would be the central point for worshiping and interacting with him. The decorations and furnishings of the Tabernacle expressed imagery connected to the Garden of Eden. It was as if the Tabernacle was to be a reminder of God's original intent for humanity. Notice the promise God gives with the Tabernacle…

"So I will consecrate the tent of meeting and the altar and will consecrate Aaron and his sons to serve me as priests. Then, *I WILL DWELL AMONG THE ISRAELITES AND BE THEIR GOD.* They will know that I am the Lord their God, who brought them out of Egypt so that *I MIGHT DWELL AMONG THEM.* I am the Lord their God. (EXODUS 29:44-46)

God repeats that he will dwell with his people and states he is their God. He's emphasizing his presence with them. Everywhere the Israelites traveled, they set up the Tabernacle in the middle of their camp, and God's manifest presence — a cloud by day and pillar of fire at night — settled over the Tabernacle.

Who was the Tabernacle for?
Was it for God?
Did he need a home?
No.

The Tabernacle was for the people. It was a tangible reminder that God was with them. They could see God's presence with them. The same reality is expressed later when the temple is built in Jerusalem. When it is consecrated, God's presence fills the temple. God is with his people. He never stops seeking.

Fast forward to Jesus. In the opening sentences of the Gospel of John, Jesus is described as "the word." John pulls language from Genesis 1 and connects it to Jesus. Then, in verse 14, John says, "The Word became flesh and made his dwelling among us." What's interesting is the Greek word translated as dwelling means to live in a tent or Tabernacle.[1] John is connecting back to the Exodus idea of God dwelling with his people in the Tabernacle. He uses the Tabernacle to introduce the idea of the incarnation — that Jesus is the fullness of God dwelling among his people. Jesus is God among the people, touching, teaching, and healing. God never stops seeking.

After Jesus' death and resurrection, he ascends into heaven. What are his followers to do now that God incarnate is no longer with them? Before Jesus ascended to heaven, he gave his followers this command,

> "Do not leave Jerusalem, but wait for the gift my Father promised, which you have heard me speak about. For John baptized with water, but in a few days you will be baptized with the Holy Spirit."
> (ACTS 1:4-5)

Ten days later, the disciples were gathering to celebrate the Jewish festival of Shavuot when a wind blew through, and pillars of fire appeared and rested on each of them. Pillars of fire, just like on the Tabernacle. God's presence wasn't just in a tent. It wasn't just in a body; it was now dwelling within the followers of Jesus. The Holy Spirit had arrived.

The disciples began speaking in languages they didn't know, spreading the good news of Jesus. God never stops seeking, and he never stops speaking.

God seeks and speaks. We're the ones that hide from him. We still fall into perception deception. We still fail to trust God. We still choose to define reality by our own desires. We again and again disobey. But none of that changes God's pursuit of us. His desire for a relationship has been true even before the garden.

> "Even before he made the world, God loved us and chose us in Christ to be holy and without fault in his eyes. God decided in advance to adopt us into his own family by bringing us to himself through Jesus Christ. This is what he wanted to do, and it gave him great pleasure." (EPHESIANS 1:4-5 NLT)

Even before he made the world, God loved us and chose us. That's profound to me. Through Christ, God sees us not as failures or people hiding in shame but as holy and without fault. We are part of his family. Not only is this something God wanted to do, but it also gave him pleasure to do it! Don't miss this. Let this shape your view of God. Too often, we allow a wrong view of God to permeate our thoughts. We see God at best as a disappointed parent trying to clean up our mess. At worst, we see him as a vindictive, angry authoritarian looking to punish us for our transgressions. Those are lies of the serpent and the outcome of perception deception. God isn't angrily cleaning up our mess. He has joyfully made a way for us to encounter him. Later in Ephesians, Paul writes,

> "Because of Christ and our faith in him, we can now come boldly and confidently into God's presence." (EPHESIANS 3:12 NLT)

We no longer have to hide. We can set aside our shame and fear, knowing that through Christ, we belong.

In Matthew chapter 13, Jesus tells a series of parables describing the Kingdom of God. There's a short parable tucked in there you can read right over if you're not careful.

> "Again, the kingdom of heaven is like a merchant looking for fine pearls. When he found one of great value, he went away and sold everything he had and bought it. (MATTHEW 13:45-46)

I've often heard this preached as an example of how we should respond to God. We should be willing to give everything in order to obtain him. That's not a wrong sentiment. The only problem is when you read all the other parables surrounding this one. You discover that the main character in each parable is Jesus and not you.[2] That means Jesus is the merchant searching for fine pearls. When Jesus found one, he gave everything he had for it.

So, what is the pearl?
Could it be you?

Jesus seeks you out and is willing to give everything he has to ensure that you belong to him. This is the beautiful story of the Gospel, and it's also found in the opening pages of the garden story. God never stops seeking.

Maybe you feel like I did up in that pine tree when everyone stopped looking for me — all alone. Maybe you're hiding out of fear and shame. Maybe your misconceptions of God have driven you away. It's time to realize the truth of who God is. The garden story reveals the good news of God's character. He's seeking us out, calling our name, and waiting for us to climb down from the tree we were hiding in so he can help clean the sap off and celebrate with us.

CHAPTER 11

GOD DOESN'T THROW AWAY WHAT'S BROKEN

To the woman he said, "I will make your pains in childbearing very severe; with painful labor you will give birth to children. Your desire will be for your husband, and he will rule over you." To Adam he said, "Because you listened to your wife and ate fruit from the tree about which I commanded you, 'You must not eat from it,' "Cursed is the ground because of you; through painful toil you will eat food from it all the days of your life. It will produce thorns and thistles for you and you will eat the plants of the field. By the sweat of your brow you will eat your food until you return to the ground, since from it you were taken; for dust you are and to dust you will return." Adam named his wife Eve, because she would become the mother of all the living. (GENESIS 3:16-20)

We live in a throwaway culture. When something is broken, we toss it in the trash and replace it. In fact, as we talked earlier about "planned obsolescence," manufacturers intend it to be that way. Products are created to be easy to break, difficult to fix, and cheap to replace. We recently had a printer that broke. It probably could have been repaired, but it was easier to toss it out and buy a cheap replacement. Given that cultural reality, I find the ancient Japanese practice of kintsugi so interesting. Kintsugi is the ancient art of repairing broken pottery by mending the breaks with a lacquer mixed with precious metals such as gold, silver, or platinum. Not only does the practice enable a broken piece to continue to be used, but it also highlights the fact that it was once broken. The gold and silver lined cracks become a testimony to the artisan's desire and effort to keep a flawed piece of pottery instead of tossing it aside. What a contrast to our modern culture's approach to brokenness. One tosses aside what's broken and replaces it, and the other sees the value of each item and puts effort into restoring it.

As the Genesis 3 account nears its end, we see a broken relationship between humanity and the creator. The brokenness isn't limited to humanity either. Adam's and Eve's disobedience ripples into the rest of creation. The damage is real and lasting. They have failed to trust God. In verses 16-20, God lays out the damage of Adam and Eve's disobedience, and things don't look good. Reality has changed for Adam and Eve. The breakdown in the relationship between humanity and God has real consequences that ripple out.

The Fall impacted not just humanity but all of creation as well. There is no doubt that we see the impact of sin and brokenness in every person and every system on the planet. Bad news indeed.

What will God do with a broken relationship with humanity? Are Adam and Eve even worthy to be God's partners?

We have a tendency to read these passages and focus solely on the negative results. We focus on the damage of sin. We see God's proclamations of curses, and we focus on the punishment laid out. It may seem like Adam and Eve have failed God and are no longer worthy to be God's partners. Perhaps God is tossing them aside; they're too broken. But what if there's a different story being told that we miss when we only focus on the negative? Are there any glimpses of hope in the midst of this bad news?

First, let's take another look at the bad news. Life is about to become more difficult for Adam and Eve. God tells Eve the process of having children will be painful, and the relationship between man and woman that produces children will be fraught.[1] God tells Adam he will have to toil in the soil to produce food. Sweat and painful labor will mark the fight with cursed land to produce food. An interesting side note: the same Hebrew word is used to describe Eve's pain and Adam's toil showing both are impacted by sin. In a broad sense, God's words describe the breakdown of relationships between humans and between humanity and creation. Creation is not as God intended. That's bad news indeed, but out of all the things that have been damaged by Adam's and Eve's disobedience, why does God focus on childbirth and growing food? Surely, other things were damaged in the fallout of sin. I find it odd that these specific things were mentioned. If you haven't figured it out yet, it's worth paying attention to the odd specific things mentioned in the text.

Think back to Genesis 1 and 2. As God was creating humanity, in what ways did he invite them into partnership? The very first commandment given to humanity was to "be fruitful and increase in number; fill the earth and subdue it." In Genesis 2, God places Adam in the garden to work it and take care of it. God gives Eve to be Adam's equal helper in the project. These words and actions reflect the partnership God desires with humanity. He desires his image-bearers to continue the work he started. They are to fill the earth or, in practical terms, have children. They are also to subdue the earth, or in other words, work and tend the earth to produce food. Childbearing and growing food are part of the partnership God invites Adam and Eve to join. Interestingly, the consequences God announces in Genesis 3 directly tie back to his first words spoken to humanity. As a result of their disobedience, the mechanisms by which Adam and Eve will fulfill that first command have become marked by painful toil. To be fruitful and increase in number will now be marked by pain in childbirth and difficulty in the relationship that produces a child. To subdue the earth will require painful toil through the thorns and thistles of the cursed ground as Adam "works it and takes care of it."

Ok, that still sounds like bad news. Adam and Eve are going to have trouble fulfilling their partnership with God. But here's the good news: even though there is pain and toil, the partnership remains! God has not abandoned them. He still desires to partner with Adam and Eve even after their disobedience! I think these specific consequences were laid out not to highlight the damage but to highlight God's desire to remain faithful to humanity even when we are unfaithful to him. Adam's and Eve's relationship with God has struggled, but they haven't lost their created call to be his image-bearing partners in the world. They are still worthy of partnership. God still desires to let them reflect his glory and goodness into the world. Even when they've lost trust in God, God still has trust in them. God hasn't tossed aside what's broken. He desires to partner with humanity despite their brokenness. Or maybe even because of their brokenness. This is a theme that continues throughout the Bible. Most of the major characters in the Biblical narrative aren't exactly examples of moral perfection.

Noah passes out drunk.

Abraham is afraid of Pharoah and nearly lets him sleep with his wife.

Jacob is a liar and swindler.

Moses murders a man.

David commits adultery and has the husband killed to cover it up.

The heroes of the faith, whom thousands look to as examples, all had moments where they failed to trust God or flat-out disobeyed him, creating incredible damage in their communities. Yet God doesn't deem them unworthy of partnering with him. It seems like God even prefers working through the unworthy, unlikely, and those on the outside. In the New Testament gospels, Jesus is frequently giving worth and value to those who seem unworthy. He declares the Kingdom of God is for the poor, the hungry, and the rejected.[2] Jesus pulls together a group of followers that society at large had deemed unworthy. Matthew, as a tax collector, was a reviled traitor to the Jewish people. James and John, as young fishermen working with their father, showed they didn't have what it took to continue in the education process of their day. Simon the zealot would have been ready to murder Romans for his cause. Peter seemed to constantly misunderstand Jesus, and when the pressure was on, he denied Jesus and ran away. These are the people that Jesus chose to represent him and to entrust with the greatest message of hope for humanity. Perhaps Jesus didn't see them as unworthy as they saw themselves or as the world labeled them. And for whatever reason today, Jesus continues to entrust his mission to you and me as the church. If you knew what I've done and how I've fallen short, you'd probably say I was unworthy, too. Yet Jesus invites me, and he invites you — with all the ways you failed as well — to be his hands and his feet, partnering with him to help bring the Kingdom of God to earth.

Would he do that if he thought we were unworthy?

There are certain faith traditions and theological approaches that emphasize humanity's unworthiness. These perspectives build off the Genesis story of the Fall and describe humanity's state as worthless, wretched, and utterly depraved. There's no doubt every human being is inclined toward sin. We all fall short of our own measuring stick, let alone God's. However, in some circles, there seems to be a pseudo-religiosity that makes us feel more spiritual the more we debase ourselves and point out our worthlessness before God. We may look at our own failures and feel unworthy and undeserving of God, but I don't think that is how God sees us. The Bible shows a God willing to partner with humanity, trusting us even when we fail to trust him. Would he do that if we were unworthy? The Bible shows the incredible steps God takes to redeem and restore humanity through Christ. Would God give so much if we were unworthy?

It's important to understand how God truly sees us. What we think about God and what we think God thinks about us impact how we respond and live out our faith. If we think God sees us as worthless, it can result in two different unhealthy responses: over-achievement or defeatism. When we don't feel worthy and valued, we can respond by trying to prove our worth through frenetic activity and achievement. We'll show God, others, and ourselves that we are good enough, smart enough, and worthy of praise. The GPA, the diploma, the right car, the right neighborhood, and the successful child all become badges we wear to prove our worth. We feel the need to outperform and one-up others to prove our worth. Other people become competition instead of allies. In the church world, we say yes to any opportunity to serve, give, or lead so we can prove to God we are worthy. We overextend ourselves and end up feeling bitter serving the church. Of course, we can't acknowledge that bitterness because that would mean our suspicions are true: that we are unworthy. Can you relate to this, or am I the only one?

Misunderstanding our worth in God's eyes can lead us to frenetic over-achievement, but it can also lead us to paralyzing defeat. If God sees me as worthless and wretched, why even try to partner with him? We can simply give up. I felt this way during a particularly difficult ministry season. The ministry I was leading was struggling to increase the number of people attending. Church leadership was putting the pressure on me. I was putting pressure on myself too — I wanted to see the ministry reach more people. The lack of growth wasn't due to the lack of effort. I tried everything I could think of. I prayed and prayed. I tried my best to motivate those attending to reach out. I held special events, hoping they would be a catalyst for growth. Nothing seemed to work. Doubt was starting to creep into my mind: maybe I'm the problem, maybe I'm a bad leader, maybe nobody wants to be around me. I tried my best to quiet those thoughts and keep working on the plan. After a long season of much effort with minimal results, church leadership sat me down for a talk. In a very gracious yet heartbreaking conversation, we both agreed that it was time for me to move on from that role. I had to admit I could not lead the ministry where church leadership wanted it to go. After that conversation, all the thoughts I worked so hard to quiet came flooding back in. I felt worthless as a pastor. I felt like I let my church down, and I had let God down. I felt like a failure. I saw no future in ministry. How could God use someone as worthless as me? I was defeated. I felt worthless, and I felt that God agreed.

Someone wisely advised me to take a day away to pray and think. I headed out to a nature preserve and started hiking. As I hiked, I began to lay out all my frustrations and failures to God — not in a reverent way, either. I walked up to a ridge overlooking a small lake and sat. I couldn't walk anymore. I was hurt, angry, and confused. I was ready to quit ministry because I wasn't worthy. I didn't see any hope for a future. I'll never forget what happened next. As all these negative thoughts were cycling through my mind, I felt a breeze blow over the ridge, and a crystal-clear thought took hold in my mind, "you are not a failure." That thought was so strong and so different from the other thoughts that had been cycling in my mind. That simple phrase was loaded with understanding. I understood that my efforts to grow the ministry had failed, but I was not a failure. I felt God's acceptance and pleasure. A sense of relief washed over me. I believe that God spoke to me at that moment. My whole perspective shifted. I realized I wasn't worthless to God. I didn't know what the future held, but I felt that I had a future. God wasn't done with me. He still wanted my partnership.

I'm thankful for that moment overlooking the lake. God reminded me how he sees me. I am worthy in his eyes. That perspective shift changed my direction. Knowing God still believed in me when I didn't believe in myself fueled me to keep pursuing ministry and to seek what was next. Your story is different than mine, but I imagine you've had failures and decisions that have left you feeling worthless and ready to give up. I hope you see God's heart in the garden story. No matter how far you've strayed, no matter how big you've failed, he isn't going to toss you aside. You are worthy in his eyes.

We see this truth in the well-known parable of the prodigal son.[3] A son asks for his share of the inheritance, which in that culture would not have been available until the father's death. In other words, the son is declaring his father is as good as dead to him. He has no desire for a relationship and simply wants to take the money and run. I can't imagine the hurt and pain the father felt. It would have certainly brought social shame to the father as well.

As the story continues, we see things don't work out well for the run-away son, and he finds himself with no money, no food, and all alone. He decides his only hope is to go back to his father to try to work as a servant. The son has no thought that he's worthy of any other position in his father's house. Jesus says while the son was still a long way off, the father saw him, ran to him, threw his arms around him, and kissed him. The father didn't wait for an apology. He didn't wait for evidence of a changed heart. He didn't wait for promises to do better. The father simply welcomed his son home. Then the son tells the father, "Father, I have sinned against heaven and against you. I am no longer worthy to be called your son." Who declared the son was unworthy? It wasn't the father. The son felt he was unworthy. The Father never once indicated the son was unworthy to belong. Any sense of unworthiness was the false perception of the son. In fact, the father's next actions reveal his heart for his son. He orders his robe and ring to be placed on his son. Those were both symbols of belonging. The son was still part of the family. The father then threw a party. His son was lost, and now he's home.

To use another metaphor from scripture, Jesus is the good shepherd who chases down the lost sheep. Sheep that have wandered away are still worthy to belong. Author KJ Ramsey wrote a beautiful poem about your place in the good shepherd's flock.

> There is no imperfection in you
> that can keep you from being included in Christ's
> flock.
> There is no brokenness in your story
> that can revoke your belonging.
> There is no bruise on your body
> that is not seen by our Shepherd.
> Because he chose to be rejected, you always belong.

No one can steal your belovedness
as a sheep bought by Christ's own blood.
No fear can take away your place.
No one can shove you out of the Good Shepherd's
sight.

Only in the light of his face can you see the grace of
your place.
This green ground is where you already belong.[4]

Could this be how God really feels about humanity?
Just like in the garden, we run and hide in our shame,
thinking we're unworthy and unable to be with God. But
God is seeking us out. He wants to remind us that his offer
for partnership still stands. God is not one to toss what's
broken aside. He sees the value and worth of broken ves-
sels, and just like the Kintsugi artist, he even highlights the
broken pieces. God brings repair and restoration, but those
aren't requirements for partnership — they're the result of
it. Wherever you find yourself in your journey, I hope you
see that you're not too far away from home. You may feel
the weight of your choices, but that doesn't change how
God feels about you. The partnership still stands. You are
worthy of God's love and worthy of having the broken pieces
mended back together.

CHAPTER 12

YOU ARE WHAT YOU WEAR

The Lord God made garments of skin for Adam and his wife and clothed them. (GENESIS 3:21)

Mark Twain once quipped, "Clothes make the man. Naked people have little or no influence in society." His joke may have been more accurate than he realized. In 2012, a series of experiments concluded that clothing has a tangible impact on brain performance. Researchers coined the term "enclothed cognition" to describe how our perceptions of the clothing we wear impact cognition. In one study, they had participants wear identical white coats and perform a series of tests to determine attentiveness and other cognitive abilities. The participants were randomly divided into two groups. One group was told the coat they were wearing was a doctor's coat. The other group was told the coat they were wearing was a painter's smock. The results of the test were interesting. Those who thought they were wearing a doctor's coat outperformed those who thought they were wearing a painter's smock.[1] Apparently, clothes do make the man, or at least our associations connected to the clothing we wear, have an impact on us. I don't know all the science behind this study, but in my mind, these findings are connected to the power of identity. How we see ourselves matters, and even clothing impacts that.

Towards the end of Genesis 3, there's an odd detail about clothing given. We're told that God made garments of skin for Adam and Eve. There's no reason or purpose given for this wardrobe change. But, like most phrases in the garden story, once you dig in a bit, I think it reveals the loving character of God.

Mark Twain may think naked people have little influence on society, but nakedness was the original relational state of humanity. Genesis 2:25 lets us know that "Adam and his wife were both naked, and they felt no shame." We discussed earlier how this was a way to describe being fully known and fully accepted with nothing to hide. But after Adam and Eve ate the fruit, that intimate relationship was damaged. We're told Adam and Eve realized they were naked and sewed fig leaves together to cover themselves in shame.

But Adam and Eve, and each of us, were created to be

naked — that is, to be fully ourselves with nothing to hide. But shame drives us to cover up the parts of ourselves we fear won't be accepted. We clothe ourselves with reputation, achievement, and literal clothing to portray an image to the world, hoping that people won't see what we're hiding underneath.

If God desires relational nakedness, isn't it odd that he would make clothing to cover Adam and Eve? It would make more sense if we saw God trying to show Adam and Eve that their covering up and hiding is wrong. It seems like God might lecture them on his intent for relational nakedness. I would think he would try somehow to point out the error of their ways. But God doesn't. He doesn't say a word. No lecture. No correction. He simply clothes them.

Why would God clothe them? I think God is meeting them where they are. He meets them at their moment of failure and shame. Instead of trying to correct or instruct, he clothes them. God takes care of a problem that he didn't cause. He takes steps to deal with their shame. I find this beautifully encouraging. God is willing to meet us where we are, in whatever mess we find ourselves in. He shows up not to guilt us or lecture us but to change the way we see ourselves. Because how we see ourselves changes how we live.

What did God clothe Adam and Eve with? It wasn't more fig leaves. He clothed them with animal skins. The text doesn't specify where the skin came from, so this is a bit speculative, but under normal circumstances, to get an animal's skin means an animal must die first. If that's the case, then that means God initiated the first death in the garden — all done to cover the shame of Adam and Eve.

I can't help but see the connection to Christ, who is arrested in a garden and eventually dies as a covering for the sin and shame of all humanity. What God foreshadows in the garden story for Adam and Eve, Christ definitively deals with on the cross. Jesus, being the fullness of God in a human body, is the beautiful picture of God willing to meet people where they are and give himself — to the point of death — to redeem and restore us.

Jesus began his public ministry by visiting a synagogue in his hometown of Nazareth. He was invited to do the weekly Sabbath reading, and when he was handed the scroll from the prophet Isaiah, he turned to a specific section promising a time when God would bring freedom and joy to the Jewish people.

> The Spirit of the Sovereign Lord is on me,
> because the Lord has anointed me
> to proclaim good news to the poor.
> He has sent me to bind up the brokenhearted,
> to proclaim freedom for the captives
> and release from darkness for the prisoners,
> to proclaim the year of the Lord's favor.
> (ISAIAH 61:1-2)

In the initial context, Isaiah was writing about the return of the Jewish people from Babylonian captivity. Jesus, however, gives this promise new meaning. After reading these words, he proclaims to those in the synagogue, "Today, this scripture is fulfilled in your hearing."[2] Jesus was implying that he is the one who brings true freedom and rescue.

In the same chapter of Isaiah, just a handful of sentences after Jesus quoted, Isaiah continues to describe what this restoration will look like. He uses language that is reminiscent of the Garden of Eden.

> I delight greatly in the Lord;
> my soul rejoices in my God.
> For he has clothed me with garments of salvation
> and arrayed me in a robe of his righteousness…
> For as the soil makes the sprout come up
> and a garden causes seeds to grow,
> so the Sovereign Lord will make righteousness
> and praise spring up before all nations.
> (ISAIAH 61:10a, 11)

Again, God clothes his people in their time of need. This time, with salvation and with his righteousness. If Jesus fulfills the first part of Isaiah's promise, it seems he would also fulfill this part. All along, we see a God that desires to clothe people. He did it in the garden. He did it for his people in captivity. He does it for you and me today. Jesus brings the salvation and righteousness we are clothed in.

Those become the garments we wear, and just like in the garden, they come from God's willingness to meet us where we are and give Himself for us.

The apostle Paul picks up on this theme as he writes to the church in Rome.

> "Clothe yourselves with the Lord Jesus Christ, and do not think about how to gratify the desires of the flesh." (ROMANS 13:14)

Paul is challenging the Christians in Rome to live in a way that honors God. He challenges them to not live by their flesh or their animal-like desires, as we talked about earlier. Paul says to do that, they should clothe themselves in Christ. Notice the order. First, clothe yourselves with Christ, then resist your flesh. Sometimes, we get this backward, and we think that in order to be worthy of Jesus, we have to behave in the right way — as if our behavior makes us belong. But what we see in the garden story, in Isaiah, and with Jesus is that He is a God who is willing to clothe people in their need before they prove anything with their behavior.

Let me ask you a weird question. Are you more of a sinner or more of a saint? On the scale of sinner to saint, where do you fall? Most of us would likely say we fall more on the sinner side of things. Maybe not the worst sinner in the world, but a sinner for sure. That's the correct answer, isn't it? The Bible says we're all sinners, right? It does.

"for all have sinned and fall short of the glory of God"
(ROMANS 3:23)

But this isn't the full sentence. It's part of a larger unit of thought. Here in Romans, Paul is arguing that both Jews and Greeks belong in the family of God. Jews felt the Greeks were undeserving unless they obeyed the Old Testament Law. Paul argues that both are on equal footing because the law doesn't make anyone righteous or right with God. Here is the full sentence and the idea that sets up what Paul was talking about.

> This righteousness is given through faith in Jesus Christ to all who believe. There is no difference between Jew and Gentile, for all have sinned and fall short of the glory of God, and all are justified freely by his grace through the redemption that came by Christ Jesus. (ROMANS 3:22-24)

So yes, the Bible does say all have sinned. I believe that "all" means every human being. But there's a comma at the end of that phrase, not a period. Paul continues to say something pretty amazing, "and all are justified freely by his grace." The same "all" is used here as well. So, if we say "all" are sinners, then we also have to say "all" are justified by the grace God gives through Christ. Why do we put so much focus on our identity as sinners when clearly Paul's thought concludes with the truth that we're all justified before God?

There are a lot of ways you can explain justification. The Oxford Dictionary defines justification as the action of declaring or making righteous in the sight of God. Marcus Warner of Deeper Walk International explains justification as a coin with two sides.[3] One side is forgiveness; any and every sin and wrongdoing has been forgiven through Christ's work on the cross. The other side is righteousness. Righteousness is being seen as "right before God." It's a sense of the right behavior and the right relationship. In justification, we are given Christ's righteousness. As Paul says in Romans 3, "This righteousness is given through faith in Jesus Christ to all who believe." Everyone who has placed their trust in Christ has been forgiven and made righteous through him.

This sounds a lot like what Isaiah was promising and what Jesus said he would fulfill. "For he has clothed me with garments of salvation and arrayed me in a robe of his righteousness." Notice it's *his* righteousness, not our own. So, when Paul asks us to clothe ourselves in Christ, he is reminding us that we are already justified, forgiven, and made righteous. This is where the idea of a saint comes in. In most of Paul's letters, he addresses the people he's writing to as saints. The recipients are not a distinct group of morally perfect people. For Paul, a saint isn't someone who has behaved perfectly. It is someone who belongs to Christ. They are saints because they have been clothed with Christ.

Regardless of your moral failures or successes, if you are in Christ, you are a saint. You have been forgiven and have been clothed in righteousness. So why does this distinction matter? Because how we see ourselves affects how we act. It's the principle of enclothed cognition. People's actions flow out of their sense of identity. If being clothed in a lab coat can change your performance on a test, imagine what impact being clothed in Christ's righteousness can have. This is why, in Romans 13:14, Paul says first to clothe ourselves in Christ. Our behavior then flows out of that identity. Most of Paul's letters follow this pattern. Typically, in the first half of the letter, Paul unpacks the realities of what Christ has done for us and our communities. Then, in the second half of the letter, Paul gets into ways those church communities should live. Behavior flows out of how we see ourselves.

We see this same principle in sports as well. Imagine you're playing baseball, and you're up to bat. As you're waiting for the pitch, you think to yourself, "I'm a horrible hitter. I'm a horrible hitter. I'm a horrible hitter." Are you more or less likely to connect as the ball comes flying over the plate? How you see yourself impacts how you act. That's why coaches and sports psychologists have players visualize themselves playing the perfect game. Actions flow out of identity.

So, if you're told over and over again that you're just a sinner, what are you likely to do? You're likely to sin! That's what sinners do; they sin. But remember, the core reality of your identity is in Christ. You are clothed in Christ. You are forgiven. You are righteous. You are a saint who is loved, accepted, chosen, and worthy of partnering with God to bring heaven to earth. That changes things, doesn't it?

The beauty of the gospel is that God clothes us with a new identity. This isn't something we earn or fulfill on our own. It is a gift given when God meets us where we are. Then, we get to begin the process of living in that identity. Our actions flow out of our identity, and with the Holy Spirit's help, we can begin to become more and more like Jesus, who we're clothed in. This is what's called sanctification. It's the lifelong process of living in our "enclothed identity." We get to become more and more like Jesus and more and more like the partners God created us to be.

We tend to place a lot of emphasis on perfection, but I think God values the process. Look at creation. God didn't create the world in a final complete state. He could have created a world where everyone who would ever live exists at once. Instead, he started with two people and asked them to participate in the process of filling the earth and bringing order to it. In the same way, as individuals, we are not in our final complete state, but that doesn't make us any less valuable to God. He values the process. God wants us to learn to trust him and journey step by step through the process of becoming the people we were created to be. In this sense, when the Bible talks about perfection, it isn't so much talking about having no moral flaw. Instead, the focus is on becoming mature and complete as individuals, as a community, and in our relationship with our creator. The journey at hand is the lifelong process of letting our actions become more aligned with our identity in Christ. Sometimes, it may seem like two steps forward and one step back, but God is with us each step of the way, valuing the process over the outcome.

Our new identity from being clothed in Christ also changes our community. As we realize we are already accepted, loved, and forgiven, it changes how we interact with others. We no longer have to hide in our shame. We no longer need to compare ourselves with others. We no longer need to use others to get ahead. We don't have to let fear and scarcity guide our interactions. Our communities can become places where everyone is seen as valuable. The Galatian church had developed a pecking order saying that Jewish Christians were in a better standing with God than Gentile Christians. Paul writes to this community to remind them of the identity-changing power of being clothed in Christ.

> So in Christ Jesus, you are all children of God through faith, for all of you who were baptized into Christ have clothed yourselves with Christ. There is neither Jew nor Gentile, neither slave nor free, nor is there male and female, for you are all one in Christ Jesus. (GALATIANS 3:26-28)

How transformative could this be to our communities today? If we understand our true identity in Christ, it changes how we see others as well. When we're all clothed in Christ, we are all on equal footing and, therefore, all one — even with our distinctions remaining. What Paul is insinuating with this statement is that the most important identifier is the truth that you have been clothed with Christ. This reality doesn't produce a new homogenous group. The Jewish Christians didn't stop being Jewish. The Gentile Christians didn't stop being Gentile. But they were first and foremost followers of Christ. That identity changes everything about you and brings you into unity with anyone else following Jesus. We're Christians first, black, white, or Hispanic second. We're Christians first, Republican or Democrat second. We're Christians first. Any other identity is shaped by being clothed in Christ. We are all one in Christ Jesus.

A key part of living as God's trusted partner is to trust your true identity in Christ. God meets you where you are and clothes you in himself. Sin, shame, and unworthiness are not who you are. You are clothed in Christ. You are forgiven, accepted, gifted, righteous, chosen, loved, and empowered to reflect God's goodness into your community. That kind of clothing will change the world.

CHAPTER 13

HEAD CRUSHERS

So the LORD God said to the serpent, "Because you have done this, "Cursed are you above all livestock and all wild animals! You will crawl on your belly and you will eat dust all the days of your life. And I will put enmity between you and the woman, and between your offspring and hers; he will crush your head, and you will strike his heel." (GENESIS 3:14-15)

I enjoy a movie with an unexpected twist. Those "didn't see it coming" moments stick with you. They were dead! He is Luke's father! He was in the room the whole time! They're the same person! (If you know, you know.) Even though we're often caught by surprise, a good movie doesn't drop the "didn't see it coming" moments out of nowhere.

If you go back and watch the movie again, you realize the twist was not only hinted at throughout the movie, but the plot was intentionally building to that point. Seemingly random details at the moment turn out to be key factors in the storyline.

To a certain extent, the Bible operates in a similar way. Small details get built upon and developed through the big picture of the biblical story. In the Garden of Eden story, we see hints that point to future ways God will move. These glimpses reveal a God we can trust working to redeem humanity.

One of the clearest glimpses of future hope is seen in God's response to the serpent. The first thing to notice is that God reveals a tension that will continue to play out for generations between the offspring of the serpent and the offspring of the women. In other words, Adam and Eve won't be the last people to be deceived by a serpent. Future humans will continue to face this battle. Will we trust God or trust our own appetites? But then God concludes his curse on the serpent with an interesting statement, "He will crush your head, and you will strike his heel." God's words to the serpent leave us looking for this future offspring of Eve who might put an end to the serpent's schemes.

Christian scholars identify this promise in Genesis as the *protoevangelium*, or "first gospel." Even as God is laying out the consequences of Adam and Eve's sin, he is not abandoning his partners. God promises to proactively end the chaos caused by the serpent. God will bring victory. But how is this battle won?

The Jewish people believed God's promise would be fulfilled by the Messiah, or anointed one. The promise hinted at in the garden story was expounded on by prophets like Isaiah and Ezekiel while the Jewish people were exiled to Babylon. They believed God's promise of deliverance and looked eagerly for one that might crush the head of the serpent — who they saw as their occupiers and oppressors.[1] By the time of the first century, the Jewish people had faced occupation from a series of powerful nations: Babylon, Persia, Greece, and now Rome. There was a growing desire in certain sects of Judaism to see this promised Messiah arrive and overthrow the occupying enemy. Defeating Rome was seen as the way God would crush the head of the serpent. Some of these Jews, particularly Pharisees and Zealots, anticipated the Messiah would usher in some type of revolution that would overthrow their oppressors.

Then, an unlikely rabbi named Jesus comes on the scene and begins hinting that he is this promised Messiah.[2] But Jesus didn't look like the Messiah many were expecting. Instead of preaching insurrection, Jesus taught loving your enemy. Instead of punishing the Roman occupiers, Jesus healed them and socialized with Roman sympathizers like tax collectors. Instead of leading the Jewish people to deliverance from Rome, Jesus was delivered to Roman soldiers and was crucified. In the minds of many, Jesus clearly wasn't the Messiah he hinted. He was killed before any sort of revolution or deliverance could happen. Jesus dies, and his followers scatter. The Jesus movement seemingly ends in defeat.

But we know the story didn't end there. Three days later, the disciples meet a risen Jesus face to face! Here is perhaps the greatest plot twist ever. What looked like defeat and another victory for the forces of the serpent was the very mechanism through which God fulfilled his promise from the Garden of Eden. Jesus crushes the serpent by dying on the cross and rising from the grave. Death brings life. What looks like a loss is a victory. And the power of sin, death, and shame is rendered impotent by Jesus' act of sacrificial love. What seemed like the serpent's deadly heel strike was actually a crushing blow to its head. Jesus took on our shame, disobedience, and curse to fully restore our intimate, trust-filled relationship with our creator.

In some ways, Jesus' approach to victory is as counter-intuitive today as it was in the first century. How can loss bring victory? How is sacrificial love more powerful than military might? The Greek thinkers in Corinth wrestled with this same tension. Paul writes to them saying,

> For the message of the cross is foolishness to those who are perishing, but to us who are being saved, it is the power of God. (1 CORINTHIANS 1:18)

Paul declares the cross is where the power of God is fully displayed. If you want to know what God's power looks like, look to the cross. Too often, we confuse God's power with the world's idea of power, thinking that force, coercion, wealth, and success create power. Yet the plot twist of the gospel shows it is in the humility of the cross that God's power is most beautifully displayed. We call hurricanes and tornadoes "acts of God," but the true power of God is best seen not in immense movements of nature but in the love and sacrifice of the cross.

I had a friend in college who practiced Judo. When he first told me he did Judo, I was impressed. I had a mental image of him doing the crane kick from Karate Kid or other elaborate punches to defeat his opponents with a violent flourish. But he explained to me that Judo isn't about kicks and punches. The goal is to throw or pin your opponent. He described a counter-intuitive strategy of Judo is to actually yield to your opponent's force. Instead of counteracting their force with your own matching force, you use your opponent's force against them. You find a way to leverage their momentum to throw them off balance. You yield to overcome.

This is the counter-intuitive move Jesus makes on the cross. He yields to overcome. Jesus' submission to the cross displays the power of God and crushes the head of the serpent. The power of the cross reverses the steps Adam and Eve took away from God in the garden.

Rich Villodas, pastor of New Life Fellowship in Queens, points out ways Good Friday reverses the Garden of Eden.

- Jesus goes to the garden to be obedient to the Father, undoing Adam and Eve's disobedience in the garden.
- Adam and Eve hide behind a tree, naked and covered in shame. Jesus hangs on a tree naked and conquers shame.
- Adam's and Eve's sin ushered a curse of thorns. Jesus wears a crown of thorns as he ushered in salvation.[3]

Jesus doesn't just reverse the steps Adam and Eve took from God. He also amplifies the steps God took *toward* Adam and Eve. Every step toward humanity we see God take in the Garden of Eden is accomplished to its fullest on the cross.

- God sought Adam and Eve while they were hiding in shame. Jesus finds us, his lost sheep, and removes our shame.
- God clothed Adam and Eve with animal skins. Jesus clothes us with his righteousness.
- God affirms Adam and Eve's partnership even while they face the consequences of their disobedience. Jesus makes us part of his body, the church, and gives us the Holy Spirit to empower our partnership.

As a Christian, I believe Jesus is the fulfillment of the promise God gives in Genesis 3:15; He is Eve's offspring who will crush the head of the serpent.

One of my favorite paintings to look at around Christmas is the painting of Eve and Mary by Sister Grace Remington of the Cistercian Sisters of the Mississippi Abbey.

"Mary and Eve" by Sr. Grace Remington, OCSO,
of the Cistercian Sisters of the Mississippi Abbey

Sister Grace drew this with crayon and pencil, and I think the symbolism is captivating. Every time I look at it, I notice new things. Eve, dejected and weighed down by her failure to trust God in the garden, is comforted by Mary, pregnant with the promised Messiah. Eve carries shame, while Mary

127

carries salvation. Eve, who was led by her desire to take the fruit, is now led by Mary's hand to touch her future hope. However, most recently, I noticed the serpent still clutching Eve even while its head is being crushed.

I find this to be a fitting metaphor for the current state we find ourselves in. Let's be honest. It sure feels like the serpent is still at work. If Jesus defeated death and sin on the cross, why is there still so much brokenness in the world?

With his death and resurrection, Jesus defeated the power of Satan and inaugurated the Kingdom of God on earth, but this kingdom isn't fully established. It's a "now, but not yet" kingdom. The war has been won, but there are still enemy cells holding territory. The serpent is still grasping what it can. How will the Kingdom of God advance and bring freedom from the enemy?

The apostle Paul closes out his letter to the Romans with an allusion back to the garden story. As you read, notice all the language that ties back to what we've talked about.

> I urge you, brothers and sisters, to watch out for those who cause divisions and put obstacles in your way that are contrary to the teaching you have learned. Keep away from them. For such people are not serving our Lord Christ but their own appetites. By smooth talk and flattery, they deceive the minds of naive people. Everyone has heard about your obedience, so

I rejoice because of you, but I want you to be wise
about what is good and innocent about what is evil.
The God of peace will soon crush Satan under your
feet. (ROMANS 16:17-20)

Causing divisions. Serving our own appetites. Deceiving
minds. Being wise about good and innocent of evil. Crushing Satan. All these phrases are referencing the Garden
of Eden. But there is one detail in that last sentence that
caught my attention. "The God of peace will soon crush
Satan under *your* feet."

Whose feet?
Your feet.

Paul says God will use the Christians of Rome to crush
Satan. I think that is true for all followers of Jesus everywhere. We are serpent crushers. This is why we need to be
reminded of God's original invitation to partnership. God
desires an intimate, trust-filled relationship with humanity
made fully possible through Jesus' self-sacrificial victory.
We are invited to partner with God to restore what was lost
in the Garden of Eden by furthering the Kingdom of God
against the last-ditch grasp of Satan to deceive and damage
humanity. Jesus works through each of us to accomplish his
will on earth as it is in heaven. But through Christ, we are
not only partners. We are also his body. We are the body
of Christ. We are his hands and his *feet* — feet that crush
the head of the serpent. Jesus is the serpent crusher, but as

his body, we are serpent crushers as well. Jesus desires to work through his body, the church, to further his kingdom. What an incredible invitation!

But let us not forget how Jesus achieved victory. It was through self-sacrificial love displayed on the cross and the new life of resurrection that Jesus brought an end to sin and death. That same humility, grace, and self-sacrificial love must mark every action of those in the body of Christ. Too often, the church is quick to adopt the power structures of the world, thinking there must be a better way to advance the Kingdom of God. But we can't expect to crush the serpent with its own tactics. We must yield to overcome. We must love our enemies. We we must forgive. We must live open-handed and generously. We must seek peace. The Jesus way seems foolish to the ways of the world, but we must trust the truth that "love never fails."

CHAPTER 14

THE GOOD NEWS OF BEING BANNED

And the Lord God said, "The man has now become like one of us, knowing good and evil. He must not be allowed to reach out his hand and take also from the tree of life and eat, and live forever." So the Lord God banished him from the Garden of Eden to work the ground from which he had been taken. After he drove the man out, he placed on the east side of the Garden of Eden cherubim and a flaming sword flashing back and forth to guard the way to the tree of life. (GENESIS 3:22-23)

There are lots of good reasons people get banned from stores or restaurants. A thread on the social media site Reddit asked people why they got banned from a place. Most of the replies are what you'd expect: stealing something or causing a scene. One person tried to make under-the-table sales on used college textbooks while people were in line to check out…at the college bookstore! Another was banned from their local library after wrestling around and accidentally knocking down several bookshelves. My favorite story was someone claiming their uncle was banned from a local diner for completing their "eat a 72oz steak in under an hour challenge" six times in two weeks. That guy is committed to his steak![1]

As Genesis 3 comes to a close, we see Adam and Eve are banned from Eden. Often, when the garden story is retold, the idea is conveyed that being banished is a punishment for sin. The ending is often summarized by saying something like, "Adam and Eve sinned so God kicked them out of the garden." Both those statements are true. Adam and Eve sinned. God banished them from the Garden of Eden. But the question is why? Was it punishment for sin, or were there other intentions?

After eating the fruit, God acknowledges that Adam and Eve now know good *and* evil. As we discussed earlier, the Biblical idea of knowing is experiential. Previously, Adam and Eve only experienced good. Now, they have experienced the pain of evil as well. Adam and Eve have experienced a broken relationship with their creator and with each other. This tidal wave of brokenness will continue to wash out into the rest of creation, leaving death in its wake. This brokenness is the current reality for Adam and Eve.

With that new broken reality in mind, God says that humanity must not be allowed to eat from the tree of life and live forever. This is an interesting shift. Adam and Eve were permitted to eat from this tree up until this point. It was never off-limits. So why does God want them not to eat from it now? I think it's because God doesn't want Adam and Eve to live forever in their current state of brokenness. God never intended for humanity to experience evil. Now that humanity has, God doesn't want humanity to live in this miserable state forever. Banishment from the garden is not a harsh punishment but another beautiful act of mercy by God. He will not let humanity live in a state of eternal misery with no other option. This act of mercy sets up a glimpse of God's plan to keep brokenness, sin, and death from having the last say among his image-bearing partners.

Speaking of partners, did you notice God mentioned that Adam would continue to work the ground outside the garden? This is another reminder that despite all that sin has broken, it hasn't broken God's invitation for partnership. He still desires to partner with humanity to shape the world and begin to bring repair to what has been broken.

WHERE IS THIS HEADED?

It's clear that life outside the Garden of Eden is not what God intended when he first invited humanity into an intimate, trust-filled relationship. Adam and Eve have failed to trust. Yet, as we've seen, in the midst of that failure, God hasn't lost trust in humanity. He continues to pursue humanity with grace and, through Jesus, allows us to trust again. But where is all this headed? What is God's ultimate goal as he works through human history?

We can find glimpses of this answer in the Garden of Eden story as well. There are a couple of themes in the closing verses of Genesis 3 that get built upon through the Biblical story. Understanding these themes helps point us to God's ultimate promise revealed in the narrative of the Bible — that he will redeem and restore all things, bringing the world back to what he intended in the Garden of Eden.

EAST AND WEST

After Adam and Eve are banished from the garden, God places cherubim on the east side of the garden to guard its entrance. It's interesting that a specific direction is given. Why east? That little detail will pop up again and again in the Biblical story, communicating a much bigger picture of God's mercy.

As you keep reading Genesis, East comes up a few more times.

- After Cain kills his brother, he "went out from the Lord's presence and lived in the land of Nod,

east of Eden." (Genesis 4:16)
- People moved eastward to the plains of Shinar (which is Babylon) to build the tower of Babel. (Genesis 11:2)
- Lot moved east and set up his tents in the corrupt city of Sodom. (Genesis 13:11)

The first half of Genesis paints a picture of humanity moving further and further east. Nearly every reference to the East is connected to choices humanity makes to move step after step away from God's ideal.

But God doesn't just let his sheep wander off. As we discussed earlier, he is always seeking and speaking. If moving east symbolized moving away from God, then moving west would symbolize moving toward God. We see in scripture several ways that God makes a way back "from the east" toward his presence.

When the Israelites were wandering in the desert, God gave them the Tabernacle as a reminder of his presence with them. The Tabernacle had all kinds of symbolism pointing back to the Garden of Eden. It's interesting, then, that the entrance to the Tabernacle faced east, just like the entrance to the garden. So, to enter into God's presence in the Tabernacle, people had to come from the East and head west. When the Israelites entered God's promised land, they crossed the Jordan River from the East, heading west into the promised land. When the people of Judah were exiled, they were taken east to captivity in Babylon. Later, when they were able to return, they came back to rebuild Jerusalem, heading west. The prophet Ezekiel plays off this directional symbolism as he brings a message of hope to those exiled in Babylon. He describes a rebuilt temple and how God's presence will fill it.

> Then the man brought me to the gate facing east, and I saw the glory of the God of Israel coming from the East… The glory of the Lord entered the temple through the gate facing east. Then the Spirit lifted me up and brought me into the inner court, and the glory of the Lord filled the temple. (EZEKIEL 43:1-2, 4-5)[2]

Ezekiel describes the glory of God moving west and returning to the temple building of the directional symbolism of Genesis.

The Bible is clear that Jesus will one day return to fully establish the Kingdom of God. His return will bring about the full redemption and restoration of the world. I don't think it's a coincidence then that Jesus describes his return as coming from the East.

> For as lightning that comes from the East is visible even in the West, so will be the coming of the Son of Man. (MATTHEW 24:27)

Don't miss this symbolism. Jesus is coming from the East — from the place of our disobedience. He is heading west, ultimately fulfilling the promises of God. Jesus' return will make heaven and earth one, and humanity will be back in God's presence in the new Jerusalem, a garden of Eden-like city.[3]

The first directional detail in the garden story is a clue to symbolism in the larger biblical story. East symbolizes moving away from God towards death. West symbolizes moving towards God's promises and restoration. These directional details are beautiful reminders of God's character. He doesn't abandon his creation in brokenness, but he is moving through history to bring restoration. This story is headed somewhere.

GATES

Another interesting detail in the closing of the garden story is the placement of cherubim to guard the entrance of the garden. Ancient cities were protected by walls and gates. If someone were to enter a city, it had to be through a gate. In times of conflict, the city gates could be shut, and armed soldiers would be posted outside each gate to keep the enemy out. This seems to be the imagery depicted with cherubim at the gates of the garden. The gates are closed, and it seems as if humanity is forever cut off from the tree of life. Is there any hope of returning to God's ideal?

Ancient Jerusalem, like many ancient cities, was surrounded

by a wall for protection. Its gates were most likely shut tight when armies from Babylon laid siege in the late 500s BCE. Unfortunately, the wall and gates of Jerusalem didn't hold, and the Babylonians looted the city, destroyed the temple, and hauled away many of the Jewish citizens to Babylon. It's to these Babylonian exiles, who understand the importance of gates that the prophet Isaiah speaks a message of future hope. He describes the people as the restored city of Jerusalem. Pay attention to how gates are described.

> Your gates will be open continually; They will not be closed day or night, so that men may bring you the wealth of the nations, with their kings led in procession... No longer will violence be heard in your land, nor ruin or destruction within your borders, but you will call your walls Salvation and your gates Praise. The sun will no more be your light by day, nor will the brightness of the moon shine on you, for the Lord will be your everlasting light, and your God will be your glory. (ISAIAH 60:11, 18-19)

Gates that are continually open?
How will they protect themselves?

Open gates are only possible if there's no need to keep any-one out. Isaiah paints a picture of peace where there will be no violence in the land and God's presence will be light to the people.

Later in writing Revelation, John employs Isaiah's imagery to describe the future hope for all humanity as God brings heaven to earth.

> One of the seven angels who had the seven bowls full of the seven last plagues came and said to me, "Come, I will show you the bride, the wife of the Lamb." And he carried me away in the Spirit to a mountain great and high, and showed me the Holy City, Jerusalem, coming down out of heaven from God. It shone with the glory of God, and its brilliance was like that of a very precious jewel, like a jasper, clear as crystal. It had a great, high wall with twelve gates and with twelve angels at the gates. (REVELATION 21:9-12)

Twelve angels guarding the gates? It sounds like no one is getting into that city, doesn't it? But as we read on, we see a different picture.

> I did not see a temple in the city because the Lord God Almighty and the Lamb are its temple. The city does not need the sun or the moon to shine on it, for the glory of God gives it light, and the Lamb is its lamp. The nations will walk by its light, and the kings of the earth will bring their splendor into it. On no day will its gates ever be shut, for there will be no night there. The glory and honor of the nations will be brought into it. (REVELATION 21:22-26)

Just like in Isaiah's words of hope, John tells us the new Eden, the future dwelling place of God, and humanity will have *open* gates. Anyone is able to enter. There are no banishments from this city. Jesus (who described himself as the gate that leads to salvation)[4] has made it possible for all to find their way back to God's presence, just as in the garden of Eden. The first banishment was to keep Adam and Eve from eating the Tree of Life and living in a broken state forever. Jesus has redeemed and repaired humanity's relationship with God, and now all are invited into God's new garden.

As John continues describing the new Jerusalem, he gives another call back to the garden story. He references the Tree of Life, which was once the reason Adam and Eve were banned from the garden. Now, how is it described?

> Then the angel showed me the river of the water of life, as clear as crystal, flowing from the throne of God and of the Lamb down the middle of the great street of the city. On each side of the river stood the tree of life, bearing twelve crops of fruit, yielding its fruit every month. And the leaves of the tree are for the healing of the nations. No longer will there be any curse. (REVELATION 22:1-3)

The Tree of Life will once again be free for humanity to enjoy. Its leaves will provide the healing of the nations. The relational brokenness caused by distrust and disobedience is the basis for so much conflict across the globe. But the beautiful promise of God is that there will be an end to conflict, and healing will happen. The Tree of Life will bring healing to all the nations.

These are beautiful promises that bring a glimpse of the garden full circle. God's banishment of Adam and Eve from the garden may seem harsh, but it is an act of mercy that blooms into a new reality. It reveals the future hope that God will bring about a complete restoration of all that is broken. Heavenly gates will swing open as the new holy city brings the hope of the Garden of Eden into full reality. Humanity and God will experience the intimate, trust-filled relationship originally intended. Relationships among humanity will be free of fear, shame, and conflict. We will all experience life to the full. With this promise in mind, we see Adam and Eve's banishment from the garden as an act of mercy that provides a glimpse into the future hope that God will not stand by letting humanity remain in brokenness but will provide a way to redeem and restore all things. That is something worth putting your trust in.

CHAPTER 15

TRUST FOUNDATION

In college, I spent two summers pouring concrete basements and crawl spaces. It was dirty, sweaty work. I was the new guy and got all the grunt jobs, but I found satisfaction in building something that would become someone's home. At first, I didn't realize how important the work was. I just viewed it as setting up forms and pouring in concrete. But eventually, I understood it was more than just a concrete wall. We were building a foundation that would support the floor, walls, roof, and everything else that would turn the house into a home. It was crucial to build the foundation well. The measurements had to be exact, and the foundation structurally sounds because everything else would be built off those basement and crawl space walls.

The Garden of Eden story is part of the foundation for the Biblical story. As we've been discovering, many of the themes that are introduced in Genesis 3 are referenced and built upon through the Old and New Testaments. The foundation of God's character is also laid as we discover how he interacts with his creation. This story matters because it is foundational to knowing God and understanding his word. If we want to do our best to truly know the complexities and nuances of these stories, we must go beyond the Sunday school flannel graph rendition many of us grew up with. If the Garden of Eden story is foundational to the Biblical story, we want to be sure we get the foundation right.

As I shared at the beginning of this book, I think too often our understanding of the Garden story is limited, focusing mostly on the bad news of the Fall while ignoring the good news the story reveals. That's like trying to build a house on half a foundation. We're missing key truths the Genesis account is trying to communicate. When we miss these truths of God's character, our shaky foundation makes us more susceptible to perception deception and the chain reaction of distrust, disobedience, and the damage that ensues.

I wonder if that is why trusting God can be so challenging for many of us. Perhaps we aren't so sure God is good. Perhaps we've heard the story of the garden communicated in a way that makes God seem angry and distant and makes humanity seem unworthy to be redeemed. That's a crumbling foundation. No wonder trust is difficult.

The Garden of Eden story is better than that. Yes, it acknowledges the reality of sin. The story acts as a mirror that reveals how each of us can fail to trust God. But it also shows us that sin is not the beginning or the end of the story. It is an intruder in God's good story, and it's one that He moves heaven and earth to free us from. Sin was never meant to be our defining identity. I hope some of the discoveries we made together have strengthened your trust foundation. I pray the truths of God's character revealed in the garden story become a firm foundation you continue to build upon as you learn to trust God more and more. May you hold these truths close and remember them often.

Remember that God's story starts in goodness and abundance. God is faithful and worthy of trust.

When you do fail to trust God and pull away in shame and fear, remember that God is always seeking and speaking. God is faithfully pursuing you, making a way back to the right relationship. He never pulls away, and he never stops seeking you.

Remember that even when you've lost trust in God, God still has trust in you. God hasn't tossed aside what's broken. He sees your value and has gone to great lengths to redeem and restore you.

Remember that your truest identity is that you are clothed in Christ. God meets you where you are and clothes you in himself. Sin, shame, and unworthiness do not define you. You are clothed in Christ. You are forgiven, accepted, gifted, righteous, chosen, loved, and empowered to reflect God's goodness into your community.

Remember that you are the body of Christ. You are part of the foot that crushes the head of the serpent through self-sacrificial love.

Remember that God makes a way home for those exiled from the garden and that the gates of the new Jerusalem are always open for you to come home.

Remember that God desires a trust-filled intimate partnership with you, and he has moved throughout history to make it happen.

The story of the Bible, when built on the foundation of God's character, is a beautiful story. The story of the Fall truly reveals a God worth trusting.

The question is, will you trust that story?

MEDITATING ON THE STORY

My prayer is that this book will help you trust God and will help you discover the depths of his love for you. I hope you continue to build your foundation by reading and meditating on this story again and again. Every time I engage with the garden story, I discover new insights, and I'm reminded of God's character anew. I hope you have a greater appreciation for the insights and truths we discovered and that you walk away with a greater hunger to read and reread and reread the text.

The Bible was intentionally written to be engaged multiple times. Genesis and much of the rest of the Bible are written as ancient Middle Eastern meditation literature. The scripture we read and study was not written as a modern textbook that lists facts and concise information. It's written in a deep and complex way to invite continued reflection and thought, allowing the scripture to infiltrate your heart and mind over a lifetime of study. Some of the patterns and themes that I've pointed out in this book were only discovered by people reading, rereading, and meditating on these foundational yet transformational stories.

When I talk about meditating on scripture, I'm referring to the practice of reading and rereading the text and then thinking about it over and over. The best illustration that comes to mind is a goat chewing its cud. Growing up, my family raised dairy goats. It was a common view to look out in the pasture and see goats lying down, chewing and chewing — almost as if they all had bubble gum in their mouth. That chewing is part of the digestion process for ruminant animals like goats, sheep, and cows. These animals eat grass or hay, then later regurgitate some of it as cud to rechew and break into smaller pieces. This process helps the animal better digest the food and get the full nutritional value.

Meditation literature is to be engaged in the same way. We read the text and then chew it over and over in our minds, gaining some understanding and insight. Then, later, we will reread the passage and chew it some more. We begin to see themes and connections pop up. As we meditate on the scripture, it begins to transform how we see the world and see ourselves. It reads us as much as we read it.

So, just because we've spent time studying Genesis 3 doesn't mean you're done reading it or thinking about it — you've got more chewing to do! Keep these discoveries in mind and let them be the foundation that you build upon as you trust God more and more. Let these stories help you know God — not just intellectually, but experientially. May you experience the goodness and faithfulness of God.

.

NOTES

PART 1

Introduction

1. Marty Solomon, *Asking Better Questions of the Bible,* (NavPress, 2023) Technically, it was a friend of Marty's that made this statement which he included in his book. He's referenced it enough times it seems like his statement. I recommend Marty's book.
2. https://aish.com/48966101/ Fohrman is a Jewish Rabbi and helps bring a wealth of Jewish perspective to Old Testament scriptures.

Chapter 1

1. The same Hebrew words are used to refer to the work in the garden of Eden and in the tabernacle

(Numbers 3:7-8.) https://www.blueletterbible.
org/lexicon/h5647/kjv/wlc/0-2/#lexResults and
https://www.blueletterbible.org/lexicon/h8104/
kjv/wlc/0-1/

Chapter 3

1. I explain the Lullaby effect in the introduction. If you're one of those people who skip introductions, you might want to reference this idea there.
2. https://www.apa.org/monitor/2014/02/scarcity
3. KJ Ramsey, *The Lord is my Courage*, (Zondervan, 2022), page 31

Chapter 4

1. https://muppetcentral.com/forum/threads/statler-waldorf-quotes.2776/ This is the only Statler and Waldorf bit I remember from watching Muppets as a kid. I discovered there were many more.
2. These three observations come from Rabbi David Fohrman's work. I adapted slightly. https://aish.com/48966101/_
3. Matthew 8:5-13 – The Roman Centurion would have been considered the enemy of the Jewish people, yet Jesus praises his faith and declares it greater than the faith of the Jewish people. "Truly I tell you, I have not found anyone in Israel with such great faith."
4. Matthew 17:20
4. Galatians 2:15-16
5. Hebrews 11:6
6. Marcus Warner, *A Deeper Walk*, (Moody Publishing, 2022), page 152

7. https://www.smithsonianmag.com/history/the-daredevil-of-niagara-falls-110492884/
8. Marty Solomon uses the phrase "trust the story" to describe one of the key points the Torah (first five Old Testament books) is trying to make. God is trustworthy.

Chapter 5

1. https://www.rochester.edu/news/email.php?refno=4622
2. Revelation 12:9; 20:2
3. This whole concept of human vs. animal was influenced by The Bible Project. https://bibleproject.com/podcast/theme-snake-throne-room-son-man-e3/
4. Genesis 4:7
5. Genesis 4:23
6. https://www.blueletterbible.org/lexicon/g4561/kjv/tr/0-1/ — this word often gets translated as "sinful nature." That translation misses the connection to the animal/human tension established in Genesis. I think Paul, as a trained Jew, is playing off these themes.
7. Galatians 5:15
8. Galatians 5:19-20
9. Galatians 5:22-23

Chapter 6

1. https://www.blueletterbible.org/lexicon/g266/kjv/tr/0-1/
2. Romans 5:12
3. "Inside a safety net hospital that treats the poor

and uninsured," Fresh Air, NPR, 3/13/23, https://www.npr.org/2023/03/13/1163097934/inside-a-safety-net-hospital-that-treats-the-poor-and-uninsured

4. I've heard lots of people quote this. I believe this saying came from Josh McDowell, "Helping Your Kids to Say No," Focus on the Family, October 16, 1987

5. Joel Larison is the pastor of Bridgeway Church in Kokomo, IN.

Chapter 7

1. https://www.blueletterbible.org/lexicon/h6963/kjv/wlc/0-1/

2. 1 John 4:18

3. These ideas come from Dr. Jim Wilder. Dr. Wilder is a "neurotheologian" which I find to be an awesome title! His work connects theology and brain science in a very informative and perspective changing way.

4. Ryan, K. D., & Oestreich, D. K., *Driving fear out of the workplace: How to overcome the invisible barriers to quality, productivity, and innovation.*, (Jossey-Bass. 1991), page 13

Chapter 8

1. The seed thought for this pattern came from Jon Gordon's book *The Garden: A spiritual fable about ways to overcome fear, anxiety, and stress.* Gordon identifies "The 5 D's" (Doubt, Distortion, Discouragement, Distraction, and Division.) This seed thought caused me to see a different pattern

of "D's" that I think depict the pattern presented in the Garden of Eden story that every human goes through as we fall victim to deception and lies of the enemy.

PART 2

Chapter 9
1. https://americansongwriter.com/closing-time-semisonic-behind-song-lyrics/
2. Hebrews 4:12

Chapter 10
1. https://www.blueletterbible.org/lexicon/g4637/kjv/tr/0-1/
2. Jesus defines this for us in the parable of the weeds (Matthew 13:37). The same interpretation holds up for the parable of the net and the parable of the mustard seed and yeast.

Chapter 11
1. The Hebrew word translated as pain isn't a word that describes the specific act of birth. There are other Hebrew words for that. By using this word, the author is most likely referencing the difficulty of the whole process of bearing children in the ancient world including the difficulty of conceiving, the challenges of pregnancy, the dangers of birth, and infant mortality. The Bible Project: Does God Punish Women With Pain In Childbirth https://www.youtube.com/watch?v=h_zIJt0Kpes

2. Luke 6:20-22 – Luke's rendering of the beatitudes brings out this emphasis.
3. Luke 15:11-32
4. KJ Ramsey, *The Lord is my Courage*, (Zondervan, 2022), page 53

Chapter 12

1. https://www.sciencedirect.com/science/article/abs/pii/S0022103112000200
2. Luke 4:18-21
3. Marcus Warner, *A Deeper Walk*, (Moody Publishing, 2022)

Chapter 13

1. For example, Isaiah 14:29-32
2. Matthew 11:3-5 – In the conversation with John the Baptist, Jesus hints that he is the Messiah. The activities Jesus cites all paraphrase various Old Testament descriptions of the time of promised salvation: Isaiah 35:5-6; 26:19; 29:18-19; 61:1. Jesus may not directly claim the title of Messiah, but he clearly insinuates it by pointing to what he has been doing, which verify his Messiahship and point to the fulfillment of the Old Testament promises.
3. https://twitter.com/richvillodas/status/1644322539336876032/photo/1

Chapter 14

1. https://www.reddit.com/r/AskReddit/comments/pjd4ll/people_whove_been_banned_from_somewhere_for_life/

2. Some people see this as a messianic prophecy. Some views hold that when Jesus returns he will enter Jerusalem through the eastern gate which was sealed shut in AD 1540–41 by order of Suleiman the Magnificent, a sultan of the Ottoman Empire. I tend to think Ezekiel and then later Jesus were playing off of the symbolism of the biblical theme.
3. Revelation 21 & 22 are full of symbolism describing the New Jerusalem as a Garden of Eden type setting.
4. John 10:9

ABOUT THE AUTHOR

Brent Faulkner is a teaching pastor and connections pastor at Crossroads Community Church in Kokomo, Indiana. He has a passion to help people see the glory and goodness of God revealed in scripture. His favorite place to be is sitting around a campfire with family and friends. You can hear more of his teaching and scriptural insight on his podcast, Walk On with Brent Faulkner. Access the Walk On podcast and other Bible content at brentfaulkner.com.

GOOD NEWS IS MEANT TO BE SHARED!

If you found this book helpful, please spread the word!
- Post a review on Amazon.
- Share about the book on your social media.
- Give a copy to a friend or family member.

Thanks for reading!